BEACH BOYS ARCHIVES

VOLUME 6

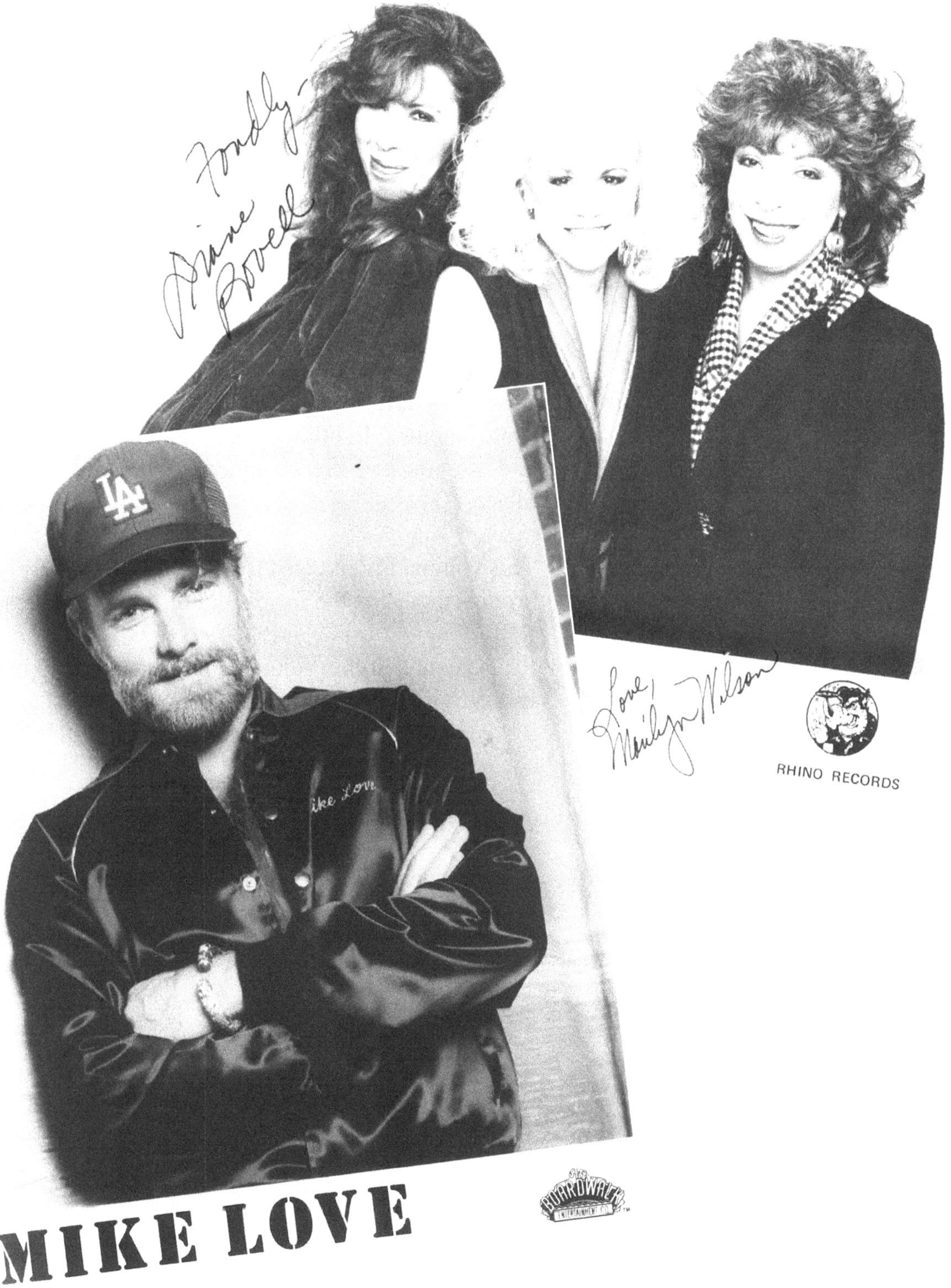

MIKE LOVE

FOREWORD

The Beach Boys are one of the most successful American bands of all time. And the members of the band, while beginners at the time they formed, matured into talented musicians.

They've been a fairly prolific band, as well. The amount of unreleased music is at least equal to the music they've released over the years. That's a heck of a lot of material in both areas. Surely, owning their own Brother Studios helped a lot.

So it should come as no surprise that the band members have also worked on a number of projects outside the formal band. In some cases, that has taken on the form of "solo" albums. In other cases, they've produced other acts and even formed new or joined existing artists to produce music.

This volume is dedicated to their work that has been produced outside the formal definition of The Beach Boys.

Please note that this volume does have some material that was also included in the Jan & Dean archives, given Mike Love teaming with Dean Torrence in the 1980s.

Copyright 2016 White Lightning Publishing

All reprinted materials believed to be in the public domain, copyright abandoned as the publishing companies have folded or we have received permission to reprint the kmaterials within. If you believe we are in error, please contact us with proof of ownership and copyright status so that the pieces can be removed from subsequent printings.

ALMOST SUMMER - CELEBRATION

3791ASMX

Words by BRIAN WILSON, MIKE LOVE and AL JARDINE
Music by BRIAN WILSON

Recorded by CELEBRATION featuring MIKE LOVE on MCA RECORDS

You and a guest are invited to a screening of ....

Almost Summer

Samuel Goldwyn Theatre
8949 Wilshire Boulevard
Tuesday, September 12, 8:30 P.M.

"ALMOST SUMMER" Starring BRUNO KIRBY · LEE PURCELL · DIDI CONN · JOHN FRIEDRICH · THOMAS CARTER and TIM MATHESON as KEVIN Written by JUDITH BERG & SANDRA BERG and MARTIN DAVIDSON & MARC REID RUBEL · Directed by MARTIN DAVIDSON Music Score by CHARLES LLOYD and RON ALTBACH · Produced by ROB COHEN Executive Producer STEVE TISCH A MOTOWN PRODUCTION A UNIVERSAL PICTURE TECHNICOLOR®

Title Song "ALMOST SUMMER" Written by BRIAN WILSON, MIKE LOVE and AL JARDINE Sung by CELEBRATION featuring MIKE LOVE

Single "ALMOST SUMMER" and Original Soundtrack Album on MCA Records and Tapes

Now a DELL Book

PG PARENTAL GUIDANCE SUGGESTED
SOME MATERIAL MAY NOT BE SUITABLE FOR PRE-TEENAGERS

CELEBRATION PICS FROM USC CONCERT

ALMOST SUMMER - CELEBRATION

K·EARTH MUSIC
SURVEY NO. 55 FOR WEEK OF 5-16

LAST WEEK	THIS WEEK	TITLE	ARTIST	WEEKS
1	1	WITH A LITTLE LUCK	WINGS	10
2	2	IF I CAN'T HAVE YOU	YVONNE ELLIMAN	17
3	3	DISCO INFERNO	TRAMMPS	10
4	4	YOU'RE THE ONE THAT I WANT	TRAVOLTA/NEWTON-JOHN	9
6	5	SHADOW DANCING	ANDY GIBB	7
8	6	IT'S A HEARTACHE	BONNIE TYLER	8
5	7	THE CLOSER I GET TO YOU	FLACK/HATHAWAY	11
10	8	TOO MUCH, TOO LITTLE, TOO LATE	MATHIS/WILLIAMS	7
7	9	COUNT ON ME	JEFFERSON STARSHIP	10
11	10	IMAGINARY LOVER	ATLANTA RHYTHM SECTION	6
12	11	BABY HOLD ON	EDDIE MONEY	10
16	12	YOU BELONG TO ME	CARLY SIMON	7
17	13	BAKER STREET	GERRY RAFFERTY	5
15	14	ON BROADWAY	GEORGE BENSON	8
19	15	COPACABANA	BARRY MANILOW	4
18	16	FEELS SO GOOD	CHUCK MANGIONE	7
22	17	TWO OUT OF THREE AIN'T BAD	MEATLOAF	3
20	18	BECAUSE THE NIGHT	PATTI SMITH	4
21	19	BLUER THAN BLUE	MICHAEL JOHNSON	4
24	20	STILL THE SAME	BOB SEGER	3
23	21	USE TA BE MY GIRL	O'JAYS	3
28	22	ONLY THE GOOD DIE YOUNG	BILLY JOEL	2
26	23	DANCE WITH ME	PETER BROWN	2
-	24	FM	STEELY DAN	1
27	25	ALMOST SUMMER	CELEBRATION/MIKE LOVE	3
-	26	EVERYBODY DANCE	CHIC	1
-	27	RUNAWAY	JEFFERSON STARSHIP	1
-	28	EVERY KINDA PEOPLE	ROBERT PALMER	1
-	29	LET'S ALL CHANT	MICHAEL ZAGER	1

Music days will be Monday 9:00 to 6:00 and Tuesday 9:00 to 12 noon...or by appointment.

Bob Hamilton
BOB HAMILTON
PROGRAM DIRECTOR

5901 Venice Boulevard, Los Angeles, California 90034 (213) 937-5230
RKO RADIO

ALMOST SUMMER - CELEBRATION

K·EARTH MUSIC

SURVEY NO. 56 FOR WEEK OF 5-23

LAST WEEK	THIS WEEK	TITLE	ARTIST	WEEKS
1	1	WITH A LITTLE LUCK	WINGS	11
5	2	SHADOW DANCING	ANDY GIBB	8
6	3	IT'S A HEARTACHE	BONNIE TYLER	9
11	4	BABY HOLD ON	EDDIE MONEY	11
4	5	YOU'RE THE ONE THAT I WANT	TRAVOLTA/NEWTON-JOHN	10
3	6	DISCO INFERNO	TRAMMPS	11
8	7	TOO MUCH, TOO LITTLE, TOO LATE	MATHIS/WILLIAMS	8
10	8	IMAGINARY LOVER	ATLANTA RHYTHM SECTION	7
7	9	THE CLOSER I GET TO YOU	FLACK/HATHAWAY	12
2	10	IF I CAN'T HAVE YOU	YVONNE ELLIMAN	18
13	11	BAKER STREET	GERRY RAFFERTY	6
12	12	YOU BELONG TO ME	CARLY SIMON	8
16	13	FEELS SO GOOD	CHUCK MANGIONE	8
15	14	COPACABANA	BARRY MANILOW	5
18	15	BECAUSE THE NIGHT	PATTI SMITH	5
17	16	TWO OUT OF THREE AIN'T BAD	MEATLOAF	4
14	17	ON BROADWAY	GEORGE BENSON	9
23	18	DANCE WITH ME	PETER BROWN	3
19	19	BLUER THAN BLUE	MICHAEL JOHNSON	5
20	20	STILL THE SAME	BOB	4
21	21	USE TA BE MY GIRL	O'JAYS	4
22	22	ONLY THE GOOD DIE YOUNG	BILLY JOEL	3
24	23	FM	STEELY DAN	2
25	24	ALMOST SUMMER	CELEBRATION/MIKE LOVE	4
26	25	EVERYBODY DANCE	CHIC	2
27	26	RUNAWAY	JEFFERSON STARSHIP	2
28	27	EVERY KINDA PEOPLE	ROBERT PALMER	2
-	28	DEACON BLUES	STEELY DAN	1
-	29	MY ANGEL BABY	TOBY BEAU	1
EXTRA		KING TUT	STEVE MARTIN	1

Music days will be Monday 9:00 to 6:00 and Tuesday 9:00 to 12 noon... or by appointment

Bob Hamilton
BOB HAMILTON
PROGRAM DIRECTOR

5901 Venice Boulevard, Los Angeles, California 90034 (213) 937-5230
RKO RADIO

MIKE & DEAN

Now! Make High-Quality Cassette Copies in Half the Time with Radio Shack's Dual-Cassette Deck

High-Speed Dubbing. The exciting new Realistic® SCT-28 duplicates your tapes at twice the normal recording speed. You get professional sounding copies and you save time, too—no second deck or patch cords required.

Two Superb Decks in One. Deck-1 is designed for playback only, and features a special narrow-gap tape head. Deck-2 has full record/play capability and a wide-gap head for superior recording results. In fact, using Radio Shack's Supertape® Metal, the frequency response is an amazing 30-19,000 Hz. And both decks feature soft-touch controls for smooth, easy operation.

Continuous-Play Function. The SCT-28 can be set to automatically play two cassettes in sequence for up to two hours of uninterrupted music.

Auto-Search Music System. Deck-1 has ASMS to help you locate your favorite selections quickly. Each time you press the button the SCT-28 finds and plays the next or previous song automatically!

Features for Great-Sounding Copies. You get Dolby*B noise reduction for expanded dynamic range and dramatically lowered tape hiss. Selectors for noise-free normal, CrO_2/high-bias and metal cassettes and a fine-bias control. Two-color, five-step LED peak meters to indicate the signal level. And a normal-speed button so you can listen as you dub. Plus, mike and line inputs let you use the SCT-28 like a regular deck.

Come in for a hands-on demonstration today and discover high-speed dubbing for yourself. Only $339.95 at Radio Shack.

Here's Mike Love of the Beach Boys and Dean Torrence of Jan and Dean

"Dean uses the SCT-28 to make copies of my songs, so he can learn to sing."

Radio Shack®
A DIVISION OF TANDY CORPORATION

Catch Mike and Dean's New Recording, "Rock'n'Roll City", Only $4.99 on Dolbyized* Cassettes—Exclusively at Radio Shack

Retail price may vary at individual stores and dealers.
*TM Dolby Laboratories Licensing Corp.

MIKE & DEAN

Radio Shack's Mach One® Speaker Sale

3-WAY SYSTEM WITH POWERFUL 15" WOOFER NOW $100 OFF!

Our Mach One Liquid-Cooled Speaker System is a bass lover's dream. You can actually feel the punch of its powerful 15" woofer and massive 2-pound magnet.

We match our rock-solid bass with exceptional clarity in the mid and high frequencies—made possible by sectoral mid-range and heavy-duty tweeter horns. A ferrofluid cooling system helps control voice coil travel for a lifelike response and increases the system's power handling capacity to 160 watts.

And with its genuine oiled walnut veneer finish, you've got a 3-way speaker system that looks and sounds like a million.

Take it from Mike Love of the Beach Boys and Dean Torrence of Jan and Dean. Dean says . . .

"I'm putting a pair in my studio. Mike wants a pair for his Bentley."

On sale at 42% off now through June 26. So don't delay, run down to your nearest Radio Shack, and experience the excitement of bass you can actually feel.

Radio Shack®
A DIVISION OF TANDY CORPORATION

Mach One Speaker System
Reg. 239.95   **Sale 139.95** each

Catch Mike and Dean's New Recording, "Rock'n'Roll City", Only $4.99 on Dolbyized* Cassettes—Exclusively at Radio Shack

* TM Dolby Laboratories Licensing Corp.   Prices may vary from store to store.

MIKE & DEAN

MIKE & DEAN

"BE TRUE TO YOUR BUD"

MIKE LOVE
DEAN TORRENCE
GARY GRIFFIN
© IRVING/ALMO MUSIC

WHEN SOME LOUD BRAGGART
TRIES TO PUT ME DOWN
AND SAYS HIS BEER IS GREAT
I TELL HIM RIGHT AWAY
NOW WHAT'S THE MATTER BUDDY
AIN'T YOU TASTED MY BEER
IT'S NUMBER ONE IN THE STATE

('N PROBABLY THE WORLD)

    SO BE TRUE TO YOUR BUD
    JUST LIKE YOU WOULD
    TO YOUR GIRL OR GUY
    BE TRUE TO YOUR BUD, NOW
    LET YOUR COLORS FLY
    BE TRUE TO OUR BUD

THE KING OF BEERS
IS WHAT THE GANG ALL CHEERS FOR
WHEN WE'RE OUT HAVIN' FUN
LET'S HAVE ANOTHER ONE
THE OTHERS TAKE THE BACK SEAT
TO THE NATIONAL CHAMP
BUDWEISERS NUMBER ONE

    SO BE TRUE TO YOUR BUD
    JUST LIKE YOU WOULD
    TO YOUR GIRL OR GUY
    BE TRUE TO YOUR BUD, NOW
    LET YOUR COLORS FLY
    BE TRUE TO OUR BUD

WE'LL ALL BE WORKIN ON A
SIX PAC TONIGHT
BECAUSE OUR TEAMS GONNA WIN
WE'RE GONNA ROUT 'EM
AND THE ONLY WAY TO PARTY
IS TO DRINK THE RIGHT BREW
THAT'S WHY BUDWEISERS IN
THAT'S WHY WE'RE SHOUTIN'

    SO BE TRUE TO YOUR BUD
    JUST LIKE YOU WOULD
    TO YOUR GIRL OR GUY
    BE TRUE TO YOUR BUD, NOW
    LET YOUR COLORS FLY
    BE TRUE TO OUR BUD

RAH, RAH, RAH BE TRUE TO YOUR BUD
RAH, RAH, RAH BE TRUE TO YOUR BUD
RAH, RAH, RAH BE TRUE TO YOUR BUD
RAH, RAH, RAH BE TRUE TO YOUR BUD
(RE-PEAT)

MIKE & DEAN

University of Budweiser
STARTING LINEUP

Name:	Pos.	Hgt.	Wgt.	Class:	High School:
MIKE LOVE	LS	6-1	165	Sr.	Dorsy High, Los Angeles
DEAN TORRENCE	LS/RG	6-1	175	Sr.	University High, Los Angeles
ADRIAN BAKER	LG/RG	5-11	155	Fr.	Liverpool High, Liverpool
CHRIS FARMER	B	6-0	188	Fr.	Livonia Stevenson High, Livonia
JEFF FOSKETT	LG	6-0	190	So.	Willow Glenn High, San Jose
GARY GRIFFIN	KB	5-10	145	Jr.	Oak Hills High, Cincinnati
MIKE KOWALSKI	D	6-0	170	Jr.	Hollywood High, Hollywood

Coaching Staff:

TOM THOMAS

GEORGE BLYSTONE

WINSTON SIMONE

RICHARD CASARES

SUSAN VOGELBERGER

Mike Love, University of Bud's talented two year letterman has a very quick release and also has great touch. Mike has that natural born ability of having great field vision. He can spot a potential pass receiver even in a crowd and no matter their size. Some of his pass completions are legendary. Among Mike's sports heroes are Terry Bradshaw, quarterback for the Steelers, "I like his hairstyling" says Mike. Joe Namath, former quarterback for the New York Jets is also one of Mike's favorites. "I appreciate a family man like Joe."

Mike also kicks all the extra points and he truely enjoys his all purpose roll. "Moving through the field, heading towards that goal then finally scoring is indeed a real thrill but then to cap it all off by kicking one thru the uprights is the ultimate for me. Then when the last ones been kicked thru the uprights there's nothing I like to do better than to have an ice cold Bud and reminisce the conquest with my buddies.

Dean Torrence, University of Bud's scrappy defensive captain covers the field from sideline to sideline from his roverback position aggressively searching out potential pass receivers. His aggressiveness has led to quite a few pass interference calls. Critics have accused him of even being to defensive. "Hey, the way I look at it is that I have been doing my job for a very long time now and I have enjoyed every minute of playing time that I have been lucky enough to be involved in. Then when I hear critics say once again, "Well that's definitly their last season", I wonder when they will finally understand that our teams philosophy is totally built on the "spirt of fun" and this spirit will always endure. Sure, maybe some of the present team members may retire someday then ultimately ending up in the Hall of Fame, but new players with the same spirit will be there to take their places. My main goal every year is to make it to at least one more Spring break."

When asked if there were any changes in the game he would like to see, Dean answers with a twinkle in his eye, "Yeah bring back tear-away jerseys."

MIKE & DEAN

BUDWEISER
PRESENTS

MIKE & DEAN

MIKE & DEAN

Rock City Here We Come

Mike Love (L) and Dean Torrence

Mike Love and Dean Torrence Are Making Oldies Sound New

Dave Zimmer

BEVERLY HILLS — If you watch much television, you've no doubt noticed the proliferation of golden oldies albums ... "Sounds of the '60s," "The World Greatest Love Songs," "Jukebox Gems," you know the ones. Well, Mike Love (of the Beach Boys) and Dean Torrence (of Jan & Dean) have added one of their own to the bunch. Called *Rock 'n' Roll City*, with titles such as "96 Tears," "Walk Away Renée," "Wild Thing," "Sealed With a Kiss" and "Sugar Shack," this compilation, on the surface, doesn't seem that unique. But when you check out the credits ... what's this? "96 Tears" done by Paul Revere & the Raiders? "Walk Away Renée" by The Association? "California Dreamin'" by the Beach Boys? "My Boyfriend's Back" by Mike and Dean? Hey now, there must be a mistake somewhere.

"No," Love chuckles, "Dean and I, and some of our musician friends from the '60s, purposely did songs we didn't originally record. We tried to keep the same spirit while adding new flavor. And, because of technological advances, we felt we could improve the fidelity, the *sound* of some of the truly great songs from the early part of the '60s."

As a team, Love and Torrence do add a new element of spark (not to mention interpretation) of "My Boyfriend's Back." Alone, Love's interpretations of "The Letter," "Da Doo Ron Ron," "Sugar Shack," and "The Locomotion" are each bubbling with summer sunshine; Torrence's stabs at "Baby Talk" and "Wild Thing" ring with enjoyable enthusiasm as well. To hear the Beach Boys cover the Mamas & the Papas' "California Dreamin'" is a special treat and makes one appreciate how the group's harmonies can still blend into an orchestra of sound without any extra, elaborate tracking. Likewise, The Ripchords' cover of "Sealed With a Kiss," The Association's version of "Walk Away Renée" and Paul Revere & the Raiders' "96 Tears" interpretations don't come off as dated attempts. It's all fresh sounding, strangely enough.

Torrance observes, "If you'll notice, the 'new happening thing' is often the 'old thing' happening again — the Stray Cats, for instance. But a lot of record companies these days are still prejudiced against what they call 'used rock groups.'"

This really doesn't concern Dean or Mike, however. Their *Rock 'n' Roll City* recording (available only on cassette) is on Hitbound Records — distributed by Tandy Corporation in over 8,300 Radio Shack outlets nationwide.

CONTINUED ON PAGE 34

Love and Torrence

"Dean and I were doing these promotional shows for Budweiser," says Love. "They worked out real well. Tandy noticed this and had already released a Beach Boys/Jan & Dean compilation. They felt our demographics were fairly conservative and connoted having a good time. So we worked out a deal to do a new project with them."

Putting the music together for *Rock 'n' Roll City* involved, says Torrence, "focusing on hit songs that are still valid today. And the artists that we contacted were very interested. There are a lot of people from the early '60s who are still functioning, have their acts together, and are building new audiences."

The fact that *Rock 'n' Roll City* retails for only $4.99 should invite even more listeners. Love explains, "For the last 20 years, we've been with record companies who don't think about keeping prices down. But a corporation like Tandy can make our music available to the consumer at a price that's affordable. So, it seems like a perfect marriage."

The new team of Mike & Dean also appears to be a good one. Dean, of course, with longtime partner Jan Berry, enjoyed a string of hit singles between 1958 and 1966. But when Jan was involved in a serious car accident in '66 (which brought on a state of aphasia — where he had to be taught how to eat, talk, walk, etc. all over again), Dean turned to graphic arts and designed several award winning album covers. Then in 1978, the made-for-TV movie, *Deadman's Curve* (in essence the Jan & Dean story), sparked a series of Jan & Dean live dates. Says Dean, "We toured all over the place. And Jan did remarkably well. When he's well directed, he can execute fairly quickly. The problem is, Jan tends to get in over his head. It takes him a long time to start and complete a song sometimes."

When Anheiser-Busch/Budweiser contacted Dean about doing some live dates last year, he and Jan had just finished nine months of road work. "We weren't planning to do anymore touring for a while," says Dean. "But the offer from Bud sounded like fun. They were setting up shows in beach communities and wanted surf groups. So, since Jan and I had done some dates with the Beach Boys, I'd been in touch with Mike Love."

"Our paths had crossed a lot over the years," says Love. "We'd even dated some of the same girls. So anyway, when Dean called about doing these Bud shows with him, I said, 'Heck yes.' The Beach Boys are such a monolith, they can't do certain things I like to do. They can't play clubs, a bunch of free concerts. Economically, creatively, logistically, there are problems. But with Dean, it's a different scene."

So Mike & Dean, with various Beach Boys/Jan & Dean back-up players, did the Bud dates, put together *Rock 'n' Roll City*, did some more "Spring Break" shows recently, and have plenty of plans for the future.

"In the fall, we're going to do some 'Be True to Your Bud' shows after football games and basketball games at colleges," says Love. "Also, Dean and I will do a Christmas record and we have ideas for about fifteen or 20 more 'theme records.' We could do *volumes* ... all car songs, surf songs, girl songs, the English Invasion, all instrumentals. And again, instead of having songs by the original groups, we'd have these groups do other songs they liked. This isn't a new concept. Country artists have been doing it for years. It's time rock and roll realized different configurations can really work out great." □

MIKE LOVE - LOOKING BACK WITH LOVE

MIKE LOVE

MIKE LOVE - LOOKING BACK WITH LOVE

MIKE LOVE

MEDIA INFORMATION

9884 SANTA MONICA BOULEVARD, BEVERLY HILLS, CALIFORNIA 90210 TELEPHONE (213) 550-6363

MIKE LOVE BIOGRAPHY

In the summer of 1961, Mike Love and his first cousin, Brian Wilson, wrote a simple tribute to an emerging California subculture.

That initial collaboration, a song entitled "Surfin'", was the genesis of THE BEACH BOYS' recording career and launched them on a musical odyssey whose momentum continues to this day.

Mike Love, as a member of THE BEACH BOYS, has been responsible for many of the group's most popular and commercially successful songs. He likes to write spontaneously and feels he's done some of his best work that way. He wrote the lyrics to "Good Vibrations" in ten minutes driving down the Hollywood Freeway to the recording session. He and Brian polished off "Fun, Fun, Fun" during a taxi ride between a Holiday Inn and an airport in Salt Lake City. "Do It Again" took five minutes at the piano with Brian as Mike related the good times he had on a day of surfing with an old high school friend.

Mike assumed the onstage leadership of the group early in their history and as a lead singer and emcee he has always been in the forefront of THE BEACH BOYS' media attention. Because of the enthusiasm he generates in his onstage performances and because he conducts the majority of interviews, Mike is most often regarded as the band's spokesman.

The vitality of Mike Love the performer does not end on stage. He has always been involved in the business aspects of the group and the recording industry. He has also established a non-profit private foundation, THE LOVE FOUNDATION, to help promote significant humanitarian and environmental causes in which he believes.

Mike recently set aside time to devote to a first-ever solo album project. The album was produced by Curt Becher (whose previous credits include many of The Association's hits and THE BEACH BOYS' "Here Comes The Night") with additional production help from Jim Studer. Jim contributed to both of Jim Messina's solo albums and wrote several songs for the new album.

In high school, Mike was captain of his cross country team and won medals and letters in cross country and track. The stamina and endurance he developed helped to prepare him for what has become one of the most long lasting phenomena in the music business. THE BEACH BOYS have always been one of the most active bands ever in terms of personal appearances. Besides touring approximately one hundred dates with them, still more with his own ENDLESS SUMMER BEACH BAND, and playing to well over a million fans a year, there are even "bigger and better" plans in the works for Mike Love.

As the eighties unfold, Mike is becoming increasingly involved in the video aspects of rock and roll entertainment. As creator and Executive Producer of "THE SPIRIT OF AMERICA SPECTACULAR", he coordinated the production details for the July Fifth television/FM stereo special which resulted in the largest nationwide audience for a live simulcast in history.

Mike has other projects underway designed to merge music with video. His plans include a feature film, California Beach, a major audio-visual multi-media presentation and possible Broadway play based on the retrospective song, "Looking Back With Love".

All of this activity requires an enormous reservoir of energy. Mike draws upon his twelve year background of twice daily TRANSCENDENTAL MEDITATION and TM-SIDHI program sessions and a regular routine of aerobic exercise and NAUTILUS workouts to give him the strength to stay on top of his demanding schedule.

The last twenty years have been rich in experience for Mike Love - writing, recording and travelling the world performing. "Believe it or not", Mike observes, "I think the future will be even more exciting and challenging."

He adds, "I'm looking forward to making movies and their soundtracks and to enjoying the promotional and performing aspects of the entertainment business, while trying to do the best job I can so I can look back with pride on what I've accomplished."

Mike concludes, "Ultimately, I hope that whatever influence I'll have, whether as a solo artist or a a member of THE BEACH BOYS, will be a positive one that will help all of mankind to enjoy a better quality of life physically, emotionally and spiritually."

"Whether through the teaching of TRANSCENDENTAL MEDITATION or the activities of THE LOVE FOUNDATION, I want to aid in needful areas of life. I think the highest purpose of personal success is to generate good vibrations for all to enjoy."

MIKE LOVE - LOOKING BACK WITH LOVE

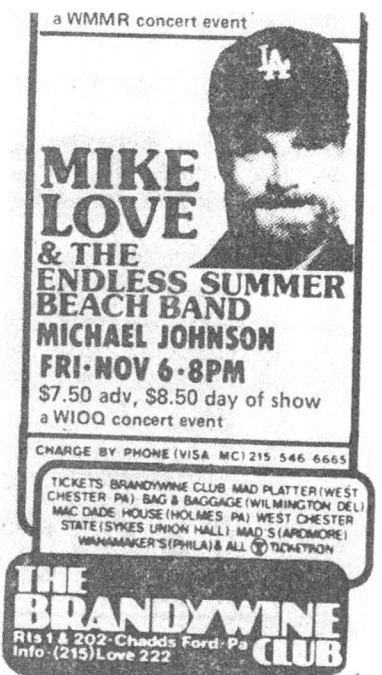

RICCI MARTION - BEACHED

Ricci Martin

- Ricci is Dean Martin's youngest son.
- His first album has been produced by Carl Wilson of the Beach Boys.
- The Beach Boys were so impressed by his writing and singing talents that he will open for them on their European and American tours this summer.
- All of the songs on **Beached** were written by Ricci except for **Everybody Knows My Name,** which was written by Ricci and Carl.
- The album was recorded at the Beach Boys' own Brothers Studio in Santa Monica, California.
- The album features members of one of the biggest groups in the world.
- The Beach Boys tour dates for Ricci are:

August 19	**Indianapolis**
August 20	**Louisville**
August 21	**Edwardsville**
August 22	**Des Moines**
August 24 - 26	**Pine Knob, N.J.**
August 27	**Charlevoix, Mich.**
August 28 - 29	**Toronto**
August 30	**Providence**
August 31	**Saratoga**
September 1	**New York**

PE/PEA 34834

BIOGRAPHY FROM EPIC

RICCI MARTIN

"Realizing that a career couldn't be served
until deserved on a silver platter, and
opportunity must not just fall unguided
in one's lap, he knew at an early age
he'd have to climb his own ladder, and
put his own residence on the home of the
star's map"

When you're 23 and have the beach at your feet, a debut album produced by Beach Boy Carl Wilson and Billy Hensche, a tour imminent with that same legendary group, naturally you're going to be up. But being up has always been a natural attribute to effervescent Ricci Martin. Actually, the evolvement of a recording career for the young son of one of the world's most recognized entertainers, Dean Martin, was more a case of "Everyboby loves a fantasy to come true sometime."

As the son of a famous performer, Ricci could have recorded at age seven had he wanted to. In other words, a simple want as "cutting a record" instead of a piece of birthday cake at any natal celebration could have been easily arranged by Dad but Ricci wouldn't have something as intrinsic to his nature as music be so easily given. At an early age Ricci discerned that if indeed music was to be his career, then he'd have to reach a point where someone would approach him and want to record his music for the quality of the music not because of his name and inherited station in life.

Realizing that a career should not be served, until deserved on a silver platter, he began preparing for the fulfillment of his "fantasy," that being to make a musical name for himself. At 11 he began by studying the drums. Repercussion from studying percussion led to a few session dates with his brother's popular group Dino, Desi (Arnaz) and Billy (Hensche). There he was playing the drums with his brother's group, not wishing he was his brother or his father but drumming up fantasies about being his own act and making his own music. But at that time, he was just kid brother who had gotten good on the drums and was being recognized for precocious talent. Kid brother was growing up, and staying up both in attitude and nights, practising and composing. He also began to notice his family permute. They were growing up too. He watched seven brothers and sisters discovering and making their own lives in every field from tennis to ice skating.

"At that time, I thought I'd be a crazy man to take a shot at doing music for my livelihood. I needed something more secure. So I thought I'd back myself up by studying cinematography." Borrowing from the language of the cinematographer for a moment, terms like disolve, fade, flashback and close-up became pertinent to the young Martin's personal life. Dino, Desi, and Billy, the group he had played drums with and hung out with after school had disolved, and his own plans of making it as a musical performer had started to fade, until one afternoon a little over a year ago. Flash back to Ricci playing piano for his own entertainment while in the company of Carl Wilson. The scene was quite informal and by no means intended as any kind of audition. Carl happened to be over at the Martin's and Ricci happened to be playing the piano.

The ivories inculcated the melody to a Ricci Martin tune called "Stop, Look Around." The tune caught Carl's attention in a serious way and compelled him to literally stop, and look around. Here was Dino's kid brother, (only he wasn't a kid anymore and he was no longer taking out his adolescent frustrations on a drum set) expressing an honest creativity which had gone unnoticed except by a few. Billy Hensche had recognized Ricci's potential and had shared his observations with Carl during one of the Beach Boys tours. Hensche had segued from the teeny bopper trio of the sixties to an integral member of the Beach Boys band and had mentioned that he felt Martin was a viable talent. Close up on Wilson's face, delighted by his discovery. Close up on Carl's ears, equally delighted hearing the tune and hearing Billy Hensche's words resurface from memory saying "Let's record Ricci Martin." Immediately Carl Wilson said "Play It Again S.A.M. (Son of a Martin)" and that's how a casual serendipity like "dropping by," made a lambent Martin drop out of cinematography school to make his life's dream a reality, not a movie. In addition to having his first album released, Ricci Martin is also going to be touring with The Beach Boys. How do you go from playing drums on a few sessions ten years ago to performing live at Wembley Stadium in front of 70,000 people. Well, first of all you start by playing in front of 20,000 people, something RM did last year in between recording. The Beach Boys were on tour in the South and during their encore numbers like "Jumping Jack Flash," and "Help Me Rhonda," they would briskly announce to hysterical screaming fans that Ricci Martin was coming on to jam with them. Of course in this kind of pandemonium no one could hear the name but this kind of experience had to be tantamount to the personal satisfaction of being, living, and playing _Beached_. He played with Dino, Desi, & Billy and he played with The Beach Boys. Now he's his own identity, Ricci Martin, a talented new discovery from Malibu, California. And what does Carl Wilson think about the finished product? He told his progeny "It kicks ass on our last album."

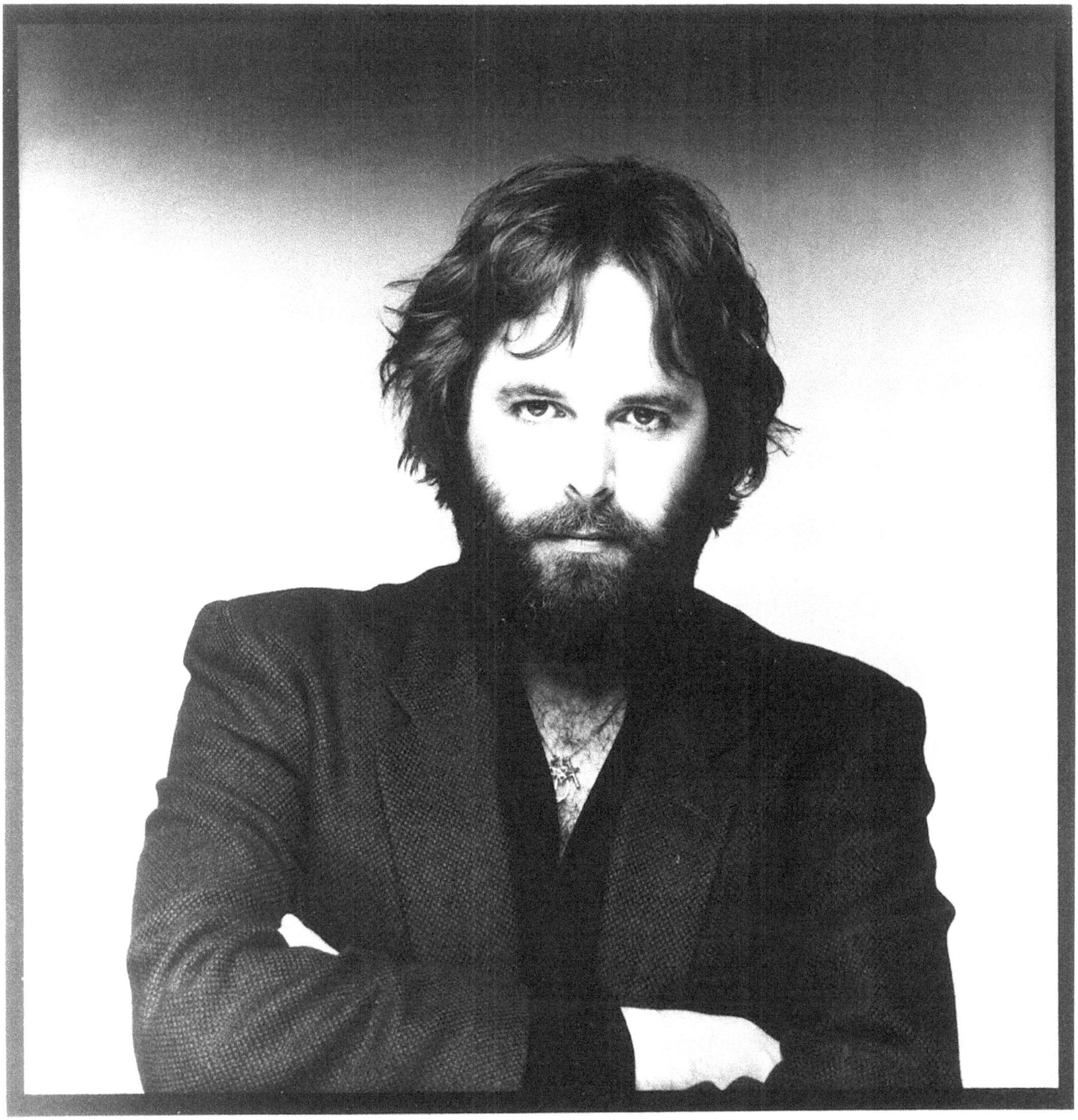

CARL WILSON

CARL WILSON

Jerry Schilling
MANAGEMENT

10880 Wilshire Blvd.
Suite 306
Los Angeles, CA 90024
(213) 475-9629

CARL WILSON

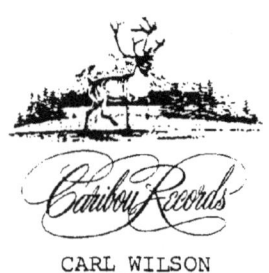

CARL WILSON

The history:

Carl Wilson's second solo album, Young Blood, advances the diverse talents of the youngest member of the Beach Boys. Differing from his early 1981 self-titled debut album in its richer production, the LP features punchy rock & roll songs that tap Carl's R&B roots, moving ballads and a spirited interpretation of "Young Blood," the Coasters' late-'50s classic. Carl's classic voice is alternately gutsy ("She's Mine," "What More Can I Say?"), tender ("If I Could Talk To Love") and infectiously buoyant ("What You Do To Me," "Givin' You Up").

Carl Wilson launched his solo career in March 1981 with the release of Carl Wilson. The LP exposed his rock and R&B influences and proved his voice could stand distinctively apart from the Beach Boys. "I feel like a part of me has been unchained and unbound," said Carl at the time about his personal need for recording the album. Carl Wilson's eight songs were written by Carl with Myrna Smith-Schilling, formerly of the Sweet Inspirations, a popular soul group. The ballad "Heaven" and "Hold Me," an R&B duet with Myrna, both became modest hit singles.

Following the LP's release, Carl reintroduced himself to music audiences on a six-month solo national concert tour. He spent three months headlining successful club dates and the rest performing as the special guest of the Doobie Brothers. During this time, Carl left the Beach Boys because of musical differences and he rejoined the group one year later, in May 1982. The man who many people credit for keeping the Beach Boys together for over 20 years, Carl revitalized the band's live concerts upon his return. A highlight of the Beach Boys' recent shows has been Carl's impassioned vocal performance on "Rockin' All Over The World," the John Fogerty song from 1975 which he updates on Young Blood.

The album:

Young Blood (Caribou/CBS), April 1983. Produced by Jeff Baxter, the ex-Doobie Brother and one-time Steely Dan guitarist who recently produced LPs for Nils Lofgren and Al Kooper. Recorded at Cherokee and Westlake studios in Los Angeles and Caribou Ranch in Colorado. Contains 11 songs including seven written by Carl with Myrna Smith-Schilling. Features musicians such as Elliott Randall, Nicky Hopkins, Billy Hinsche and Baxter and backing vocalists Timothy B. Schmit and Burton Cummings. "What You Do To Me," written by John and Johanna Hall, is the LP's first single, released in early March.

-8304-

CARL WILSON

All About: Carl Wilson

CARL WILSON has been an important part of American music for the past twenty years. As one of the lead vocalists and guitarists of the Beach Boys, Carl has been an integral member of one of the most successful bands of all time.

Carl's voice has been heard on many of the Beach Boys' hit records. In addition to his role as a performer, Carl also produced the albums *Surf's Up*, *In Concert*, and *Holland*.

This album is Carl's first solo effort. While in many ways the record is a departure from the famous Beach Boys sound, Carl is still, and will remain, a central member of the band.

Carl Wilson presents a new sound and diverse music with his familiar and recognizable vocals. This fresh new sound will no doubt open new doors for **Carl Wilson**.

JAMES WILLIAM GUERCIO produced Carl's solo record. Previously he has produced hit records by Chicago, Blood, Sweat and Tears, and The Buckinghams.

Caribou Records is very pleased to present a solo CARL WILSON.

NJZ/NZT 37010
(Caribou)

CARL WILSON

Carl Wilson solos on a little musical safari of his own

After almost 20 years of superstardom with the family group (above), Beach Boy Carl Wilson (right) is trying a first, touring with a new band. But it's only temporary, he says.

CARL WILSON

By Jack Lloyd
Inquirer Entertainment Writer

For the first time in his career, Carl Wilson is touring without his brothers and cousins. The remaining Beach Boys have stayed home this time.

"I guess I had some trepidations about it when we started talking about a tour," Wilson said during an interview before his appearance tonight at Emerald City, Cherry Hill, N.J. "But I'm really enjoying it, playing the clubs where you can be close to your audience. Yeah, in a way it's like starting out all over again."

It should be noted quickly that Carl Wilson has not abandoned the Beach Boys, those perennial rock 'n' roll surfer boys from Southern California. But he has recorded a solo album, "Carl Wilson," for Caribou Records, and he has formed a non-Beach Boys band to take this new music on the road.

But the rites of spring cannot be denied. When Wilson's tour concludes later this month, he will be back with the Beach Boys for the annual tour that will bring them into the Valley Forge Music Fair on May 1 and 2.

"You just can't stop that," Wilson said, referring to the Beach Boys' continued appeal after 20 years. And, Wilson maintains, he will continue to be a part of it. He is, in fact, considered the chief force in keeping the Beach Boys together during those many troubled times over the years when a breakup seemed inevitable.

"I've always had that role, I guess, keeping things in focus," Wilson acknowledged.

But for the moment, Wilson has his own project to focus on. It is an outgrowth of the fact that while he has remained loyal to the Beach Boys' mission in life, other forms of music that were out of Beach Boys' context kept drifting through his head.

Wilson sums them up as "good straight-ahead rock 'n' roll."

In reality, the music showcased on his album is not all that "straight ahead." There are obvious touches of R&B along the way. This can be traced to his collaborator in writing the music, Myrna Smith, who formerly sang with the Sweet Inspirations and contributes vocal support on the album and the tour.

"It just kind of happened," Wilson said. "The opportunity to do the album and the tunes came along about the same time. Myrna is a friend of my manager, Jerry Schilling. I was at his house one day, humming ideas for melodies into a cassette. Myrna started adding lyrics. The first song was 'Hold Me.' With the next song we completed, 'Bright Lights,' she wrote the lyrics first. It just kept going."

Next on the scene was James William Guercio, who agreed to produce the album at his Caribou Ranch recording studio in Colorado.

"Jim and I tried to talk some of the guys from the Beach Boys into getting off their butts to come on out and help out with the music," Wilson said. "We didn't have any luck, though. . . . Well, yeah, it's kind of hard sometimes to get them into a recording studio."

It probably worked out better his way, Wilson concedes. The s--t, using studio musicians, produced a sound totally apart from that of the Beach Boys.

Despite their lack of participation, Wilson noted, "My brothers supported me in this project completely, and I'm very happy with the way it turned out. We all put our heart and soul into it. I wasn't going to compromise with this music any more than I would compromise the Beach Boys' music."

The Beach Boys' lingering mystique is, of course, a source of gratification to Wilson, although he is a bit chagrined over the minimal success of the group's albums in recent years. "You can count on it every spring," Wilson said. "Radio stations start playing our records. Mostly the old stuff. I don't know — some of the later albums were higher quality, I think. 'Pet Sounds' was one, but it didn't do a lot."

No matter — when spring arrives, you know the Beach Boys can't be far behind.

●

The Brandywine Club in Chadds Ford has emerged as the area's newest pop music entertainment spot. Electric Factory Concerts has taken over the booking operation at the spacious facility, which has a 1,500 capacity and 11 bars scattered throughout the room.

The Brandywine will be bringing in name talent and will also provide a showcase for local performers during Wednesday "$2 nights." This Wednesday, for instance, the Hooters and the Get Right Band will appear. Then on Saturday, Delbert McClinton will headline.

Steve Apple, spokesman for Electric Factory Concerts, pointed out that the operation will be geared to audiences in the Delaware area and will not necessarily conflict with Philadelphia attractions. Steve Forbert, for instance, drew a crowd of around 1,300 at the Brandywine last weekend — one week after selling out at the Ripley Music Hall in Philadelphia.

"We'll be experimenting with a lot of ideas," Apple pointed out. "We'll try some comedy and perhaps even some dinner theater attractions that may be brought in for a couple of weeks."

WHAT THE CRITICS HAVE SAID ABOUT CARL WILSON

The First Album

"**Carl Wilson** is a long-overdue personal triumph...He's come up with some of the freshest, most exciting new music any of the Beach Boys have been associated with in far too many years."
Dale Adamson, Houston Chronicle

"This year it looks like the spirit of endless summer is residing with brother Carl."
Dale Anderson, Buffalo Evening News

"Carl's instantly recognizable, high-flying vocals are put to excellent use on an assortment of very well-crafted, modern pop/rock tunes...A very impressive effort."
Bill Carlton, New York Daily News

"The surf's up for Carl Wilson...He's ready to rock out of the age-old nice guy Beach Boy groove."
Kim McAuliffe, Detroit Free Press

"...you have to admire the guy for finally stepping out from the shadow of his older brother. It would have been easy for Wilson to lay back and rake in the money from past glories; instead, he tackles head-on the whole frustration of being a Beach Boy in 'The Right Lane.'"
Charles McCollum, Washington Star

"...a scorching hour of music." **Steve Webb, Albany Knickerbocker**

"...an excellent record." **Rich Aregood, Philadelphia Daily News**

"...the disc packs a relentless punch." **Chris Hamel, Springfield Daily News**

"...a talented rocker...one of the best voices in rock music."
Thomas Osborne, Baltimore Evening Sun

"Carl Wilson has cut a solo album that is truly outstanding...(He) is not trying to recapture the 1960s...but is unveiling a new Carl Wilson for a new generation."
Jack Kegg, Cumberland Times

The Live Show

"It was not a laid-back, 'wish they all could be California girls'-type Wilson who came to the Agora for a special midnight performance Easter Sunday. If anything, this was one 'Wild Honey.'"
Pete Oppel, Dallas Morning News

"...a surprisingly strong performance...Wilson has plenty to offer."
Don McLeese, Chicago Sun Times

"The music was tight and driving, a heady combination of rock and rhythm and blues...It was totally mind-boggling to see that familiar face fronting a band this hot and heavy."
Bob Claypool, Houston Post

"...an extraordinary lead vocalist." **Joel Selvin, San Francisco Chronicle**

"By the time he encored, not with 'Surfin' U.S.A.' but with Sam and Dave's 'I Thank You,' he'd turned the rather formidable trick of sounding like an interesting new solo artist."
Steve Pond, Los Angeles Times

"...a surprisingly strong show...more contemporary than anything the Beach Boys have done in years."
Milt Petty, Valley News

"...a strong leader figure...singing with special conviction." **Bill Milkowski, Good Times**

"...a hard driving opening set...tightly produced, high-powered new music."
Jack Garner, Rochester Democrat and Chronicle

"Although he's still very much a Beach Boy, Carl Wilson showed Sunday night that he could make it on his own if he had to...The youngest of the Wilson Brothers gave a bang-up rock'n'roll exhibition."
Roger Kaye, Fort Worth Star-Telegram

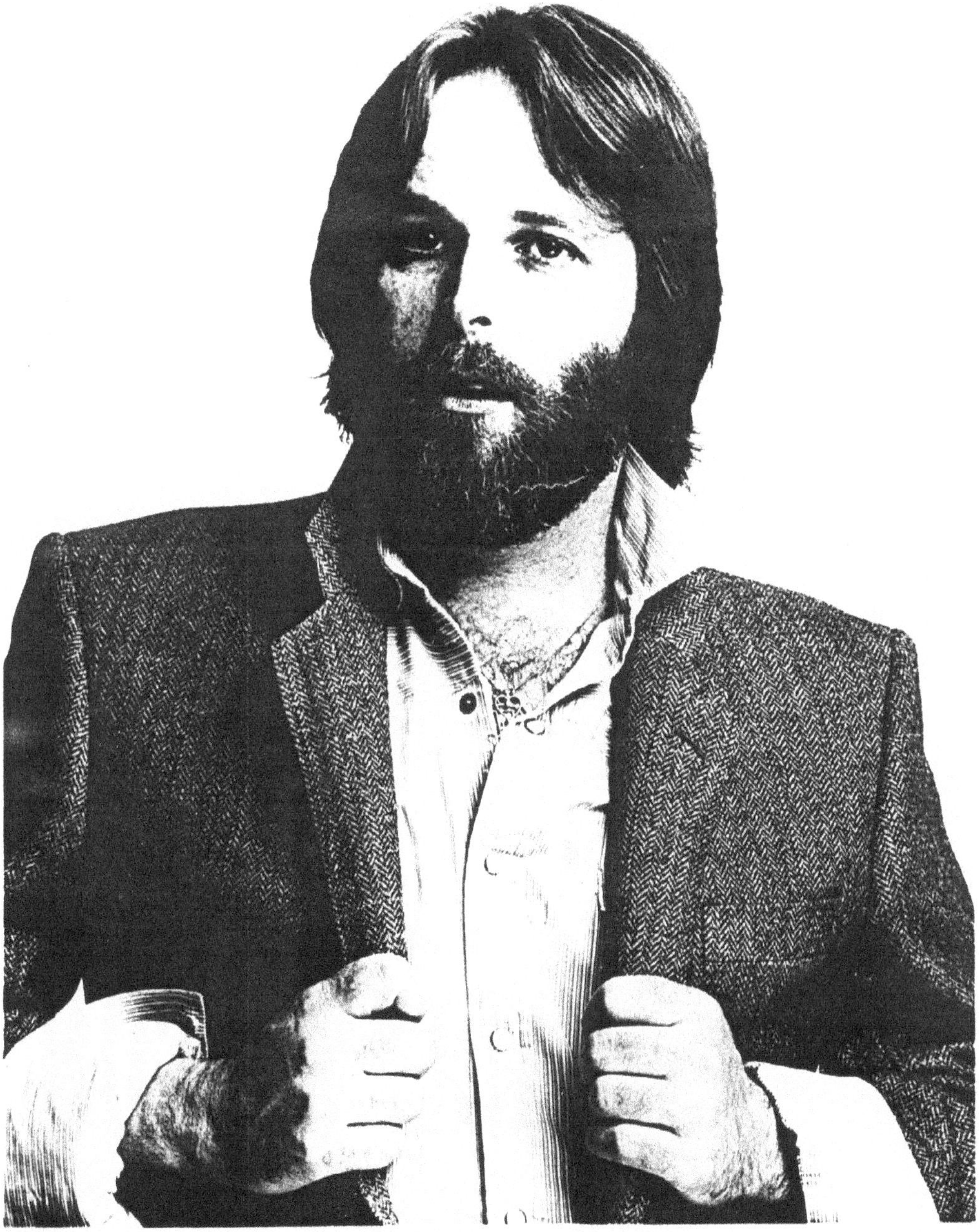

CARL WILSON

CARL WILSON

Jerry Schilling
MANAGEMENT

8860 Evanview Dr.
Los Angeles, Ca. 90069
(213) 854-0011

8207

CARL WILSON

Riding a star, a duo is born

The event was billed as Carl Wilson's show, and it is true that whenever a primary figure from a recording group that has been headlining for two decades decides to launch a solo effort, the spotlight is bound to focus mostly upon him. But the act that appeared at Emerald City on Sunday evening was, in reality, the debut of a distinctive singing and songwriting duo, along with an authoritative four-piece backup band.

Wilson, as almost anyone with even a passing interest in pop music knows, is one of the leading forces — and probably the best instrumentalist — of that long-celebrated symbol of California-style hedonism, the Beach Boys. If that, however, was the reason that some attended Wilson's show, they were disappointed; Wilson brought none of his past with him.

He did bring one Myrna Smith along, and from the sound of things — should the Beach Boys go their separate ways in the near future — Wilson and Smith would have little trouble making a go of it as a regular attraction. Smith — long a fixture with the soul-gospel group the Sweet Inspirations, who have backed up scores of performers — seems attuned to the material and Wilson's voice to an almost uncanny degree.

The reason is that there is nothing "backup" about the role Smith is playing with Wilson; every tune that the duo is now performing they penned together. The songs sound custom-made for the twosome because they are.

Appearing with a band composed of lead guitarist John Daly, bassist Gerald Johnson, drummer Alan Krigger and keyboardist-guitarist Billy Hinsche, Wilson and Smith offered songs from their new album, including "Hold Me," "Bright Lights," "The Right Lane," and "The Grammy."

— Edgar Koshatka

CARL WILSON—Caribou
6-01049 (CBS)

HOLD ME (prod. by Guercio) (writers: Wilson-Smith) (Murray Gage/Schilling, ASCAP) (3:30)

Beach Boy Wilson makes his solo debut with this single from his new self-titled album. His trademark light tenor makes a convincing plea, with backing vocal help from former Sweet Inspiration Myrna Smith (she also gets co-writer credit). The soulful chorus hook is gospel-tinged.

Craftsman Carl Wilson

I ALWAYS thought that the Beach Boys were overrated, then and now, but Carl Wilson's new solo album, "Youngblood," is a delightful surprise. For straight-ahead entertainment, solid writing and singing, instrumental support, and production (by Jeff Baxter), this is as good as pop gets.

Wilson wrote the music for seven of the cuts, with lyrics by Myrna Smith-Schilling. He sings with the ease that comes of his twenty years' experience with the Beach Boys. But there is a new exuberance behind his vocals, a feeling of release—you can almost hear him saying, "I don't have to go clumping around the country singing that golden-oldie stuff." The collaborations between Wilson and Smith-Schilling display craftsmanship and good construction, and three of them are outstanding: *What More Can I Say?*, *She's Mine*, and *Givin' You Up*. Lieber and Stoller's classic *Young Blood* is done as an affectionate joke, but John Fogerty's *Rockin' All Over the World* means business. *What You Do to Me* by John and Johanna Hall gets the Beach Boys' layered background-vocal treatment, and Wilson turns in a no-nonsense vocal on Billy Hinche's *One More Night Alone*.

"Youngblood" is a splendid piece of work. Don't miss it. —*Joel Vance*

CARL WILSON: *Youngblood.* Carl Wilson (vocals, guitar); vocal and instrumental accompaniment. *What More Can I Say?; She's Mine; Givin' You Up; What You Do to Me; Time; Rockin' All Over the World; One More Night Alone; Young Blood; Of the Times; Too Early to Tell; If I Could Talk to Love.* CARIBOU BFZ 37970, © BZT 37970, no list price.

genre of country-pop. While you're waiting for Dolly to come up with that one, "Burlap and Satin" isn't a bad way to spend the time. *A.N.*

RECORDING OF SPECIAL MERIT

JUNE POINTER: *Baby Sister.* June Pointer (vocals); vocal and instrumental accompaniment. *Ready for Some Action; I Will Understand; To You, My Love; New Love, True Love;* and five others. RCA BXL1-4508 $8.98, © BXK1-4508 $8.98.

Performance: **Sizzling**
Recording: **Good**

The Pointer Sisters made their debut approximately ten years ago with an album they have yet to surpass. I've lost track of the various comings and goings of members of the group, but I'm delighted to report that some of the fire and sassiness that first propelled them into the spotlight can be found in this new solo album by "Baby Sister" June Pointer. She has an ambitiously hard-edged tone that cuts through the background sound and commands immediate attention on the opening *Ready for Some Action*, which she definitely is. When she belts out *I'm Ready for Love*, she sounds like a Diana Ross gone wild in an arrangement that is an almost humorous take-off on the old Motown sound. June Pointer's distinctive personality shines through it all. This is a singer who refuses to be ignored, and I don't think she will be. *P.G.*

RECORDING OF SPECIAL MERIT

ELVIS PRESLEY: *I Was the One.* Elvis Presley (vocals, guitar); vocal and instrumental accompaniment. *My Baby Left Me; (You're So Square) Baby I Don't Care; Little Sister; Don't; Wear My Ring Around Your Neck; Paralyzed; Baby Let's Play House;* and four others. RCA AHL1-4678 $8.98, © AHK1-4678 $8.98.

Performance: **Incendiary**
Recording: **Good for the period**

Oddly enough, this is the first intelligent Presley repackaging that American RCA

CARL WILSON

Beach Boy Carl Wilson's Solo "Toy"

Marc Shapiro

LOS ANGELES — The early months of 1981 will not go down in Carl Wilson's little golden book of memories as his most enjoyable ones. At that time, he was agonizing over the painfully slow recovery, from drug abuse and mental depression, of his brother Brian. He was contending with the creative disintegration of the Beach Boys, a group he'd been with since their inception, and, above all, there was a 19-year-old creative itch that Wilson was just dying to scratch.

"Finally I just got fed up with what was going on," Wilson recalls. "It wasn't even a matter of me saying, 'Screw this.' At that point there was nothing left to screw."

Wilson, a bearded 36-year-old teddy bear of a man whose exuberance belies his business-like attention to detail, is making "happy talk" with the press to let the public know that the aforementioned itch has been scratched a second time in the guise of his second solo album, *Young Blood*.

Scratch One was 1981's *Carl Wilson*, a basically shy person but going solo has helped to get me out of that shell and has made me a lot looser."

Wilson freely admits that his growing frustration with the stagnation of the Beach Boys, both creatively and as a performing unit, is what led to his solo sabbatical. He cites the later stages of the group's 1980 tour as a particularly trying experience:

"We weren't really taking care of things onstage. We weren't rehearsing that much and there was just no energy in our live shows at all. There were nights when I'd be onstage and thinking to myself, 'What the fuck! There's no mystery or excitement to this anymore.' But what clinched it for me was when the group finally found a block of time to record and instead decided to sit around doing nothing. All the inactivity got to be too much so I left."

During the ensuing year, despite total immersion in his solo activities, Wilson kept tabs on what the Beach Boys were doing. And he wasn't too thrilled at what he was seeing.

"As far as I was concerned, the group really hit bottom when they

CARL WILSON

"Finally I just got fed up with what was going on," Wilson recalls. "It wasn't even a matter of me saying, 'Screw this.' At that point there was nothing left to screw."

Wilson, a bearded 36-year-old teddy bear of a man whose exuberance belies his business-like attention to detail, is making "happy talk" with the press to let the public know that the aforementioned itch has been scratched a second time in the guise of his second solo album, *Young Blood*.

Scratch One was 1981's *Carl Wilson*, an entertaining and downright surprising departure from the usual sand and surf motif of the Beach Boys that showcased Wilson's abilities at blending pop and rhythm & blues elements. *Young Blood*, named for Wilson's spirited send-up of the 1950s Coasters hit, continues in a similar musical vein and also showcases Wilson's heretofore underexposed rock and roll side on such songs as "She's Mine" and "What More Can I Say?"

"Being free to do what I want has been the most enjoyable thing about doing the solo albums," he explains. "I'm not playing to a limited idea of a lifestyle like I had been with the Beach Boys and I don't feel like I'm boxed in. What I feel like is a kid with a new toy."

Under the steady production hand of Jeff "Skunk" Baxter, Wilson has fashioned a solid mainstream rock-pop sound that is easily recognizable as being removed from anything approaching Beach Boys-style music. And nobody is more aware of the break he's made than Carl himself.

"With the Beach Boys, I was always the laid back personality who was more concerned with creating a harmonious environment within the band so we could get the work out than in developing my own ideas. But, with the solo albums, it's been my head on the chopping block and so I've taken the time and, musically, taken some chances. I've always been

There's no mystery or excitement to this anymore.' But what clinched it for me was when the group finally found a block of time to record and instead decided to sit around doing nothing. All the inactivity got to be too much so I left."

During the ensuing year, despite total immersion in his solo activities, Wilson kept tabs on what the Beach Boys were doing. And he wasn't too thrilled at what he was seeing.

"As far as I was concerned, the group really hit bottom when they headlined that free outdoor televised concert in Long Beach," says Wilson. "The sound system was poor and the band just sounded like shit. All I could do was shake my head."

Carl's return to the band last May was under the condition that the group shape up and take itself more seriously. Carl had to make some compromises of his own, however, the hardest of which, he says, was to agree to the group's commitment to a series of shows in Las Vegas.

"Playing Vegas was a real sore point with me, but I had agreed to do everything possible to help light a fire under the group so I said okay. It was really difficult going down those stairs twice a night to put on the same cookie cutter show, and it didn't take long before the group started going to sleep again. We had to revert to some real silly stage antics to keep ourselves awake," says Wilson, who is quick to point out that the group survived that ordeal and is once again cooking on all four burners.

While Wilson is not above talking about his parent group, he is candid about wanting to focus on the present and his solo adventures. And where the Beach Boys anecdotes were delivered in subdued tones, returning to the present once again brings out the enthusiastic little kid in him.

"Man, it's no more Mr. Nice Guy! Now it's Carl Wilson, rock and roller! Now I'm free!"

CARL WILSON

‘Even though he was diagnosed with cancer... he was a real fighter’

Good vibrations: the Beach Boys — Al Jardine, Brian Wilson, Mike Love, Dennis Wilson and Carl Wilson — in 1978.

1967: Carl Wilson (centre) with the Beach Boys.

1987: Wilson marries Dean Martin's daughter Gina.

1992: Wilson sings to 14,000 fans in Melbourne.

CARL WILSON

Sun sets for Beach Boy

CARL Wilson, a founding member of the Beach Boys and lead guitarist for the classic surf band, has died from lung cancer at 51.

Wilson, who also had brain cancer, died at the weekend in Los Angeles with his family — his wife Gina and sons Jonah, 28, and Justin, 26 — at his side.

"Even though he was diagnosed with cancer last year and going through treatment for a year, he was a real fighter," spokeswoman Alyson Dutch said.

"He participated in the entire summer tour this year."

The band defined the surfing sound with bouncy, hummable tunes such as *I Get Around*, *Good Vibrations*, *Help Me Rhonda* and *Surfin' USA*.

Wilson was born in Hawthorne, a Los Angeles suburb about 8km from the Pacific Ocean. He learned to play guitar as a teenager and — with older brothers Brian and Dennis, cousin Mike Love and friend Alan Jardine — founded the Beach Boys in 1961 just before the advent of the Beatles.

Dennis Wilson, who died in a swimming accident in 1983, came up with the idea of a surfing theme. Brian Wilson and Love started writing lyrics that capitalised on the surfing craze of the mid-1950s.

The quintet did not make their first public appearance until New Year's Eve 1961 at Long Beach's Municipal Auditorium. Their stage fright was not helped by the fact they could play only three songs.

Despite the limited repertoire, the audience embraced the group.

CARL WILSON 1946 – 1998

The band, known for its laid-back "surfin'" style of music of the early 1960s, went on to have a string of big hits.

Most of their albums reached gold record status.

However, it wasn't until the "psychedelic" classic *Good Vibrations* that the Beach Boys were elevated to rock superstardom.

Differences in creative goals between the quintet and its producers' led to a slowdown after 1966. The group refused to release new songs they prepared in their studio and refused to work in Capitol Records' facility.

A comeback in the 1970s was stalled by drug problems involving Brian Wilson, the band's creative force.

In the early '80s, Carl Wilson said he had tired of the Beach Boys' nostalgia and lack of musical growth.

He left the quintet in 1981 and released an album later that year.

He rejoined the group, performing with them when the Beach Boys were inducted into the Rock and Roll Hall of Fame in 1988.

– AP

VOICE of surf classics, Page 25

CARL WILSON FOUNDATION CONCERT PROGRAM

CARL WILSON 2001 MEMORY BOOK

CARL WILSON
HEAVEN'S VOICE

OCTOBER 14, 2001

CARL WILSON WALK AGAINST CANCER BENEFIT CON...

SOUVENIR PRO...

THE Carl Wilson FOUNDATION

DENNIS WILSON - PACIFIC OCEAN BLUE AD

A first. Dennis Wilson becomes the first of the Beach Boys to record and release a solo album.
 Laced with imagery of the surf and the ocean, "Pacific Ocean Blue" sings in a uniquely beautiful Dennis Wilson style.
On Caribou Records and Tapes.

DENNIS WILSON - PACIFIC OCEAN BLUE

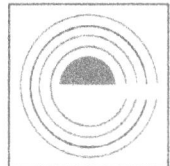

DENNIS WILSON

Dennis, the middle of the Wilson brothers, is the only member of The Beach Boys to qualify as a genuine surfer. It was his interest in the sport that started the band's climb to success in the early Sixties.

"We'd been writing some of our own songs, about girlfriends and the usual kind of things, and playing a lot of current hits and rock oldies," he recalls. "But one day in 1961, I came back from a hard day of surfing and asked Brian to write a song about it." Brian obligingly composed "Surfin'," which the band promptly recorded. To tie in with the tune title, someone at the record company decided that the band should call themselves The Beach Boys.

From the beginning until 1971, Dennis was the band's drummer. ("Denny's Drums" is an instrumental solo on an early album.) A hand injury in that year forced him to switch to less-taxing keyboard instruments. Since then his hand has healed 100% and this year he's in full swing as The Beach Boys' drummer.

In the recording studio, Dennis likes to take an active hand in the group's sound, occasionally to the point of producing songs that he has written. Brian is really the leader, but we all like to get involved in what we put down. It helps us, and makes for a better sound on record."

Dennis will become the group's first member to have a solo album, Pacific Ocean Blue, released on Caribou Records in August, 1977.

Much of the music that Dennis composes has a classical feel, which he credits to his early musical background. He has written numerous tunes for the group, including "Steamboat," "Only With You," and "Got to Know the Woman." "I usually write from experience," he says. "I find that when you're more honest, the songs turn out better."

Dennis not long ago began studying acting and co-starred with James Taylor in the acclaimed film Two Lane Blacktop. "There's a parallel between what we do as musicians and acting," explains Dennis. "What we're there to do in both cases is entertain the audience. And that's what we do best."

Press and Public Information, 51 W. 52 Street, New York, N.Y. 10019/ Tel. (212)975-4321

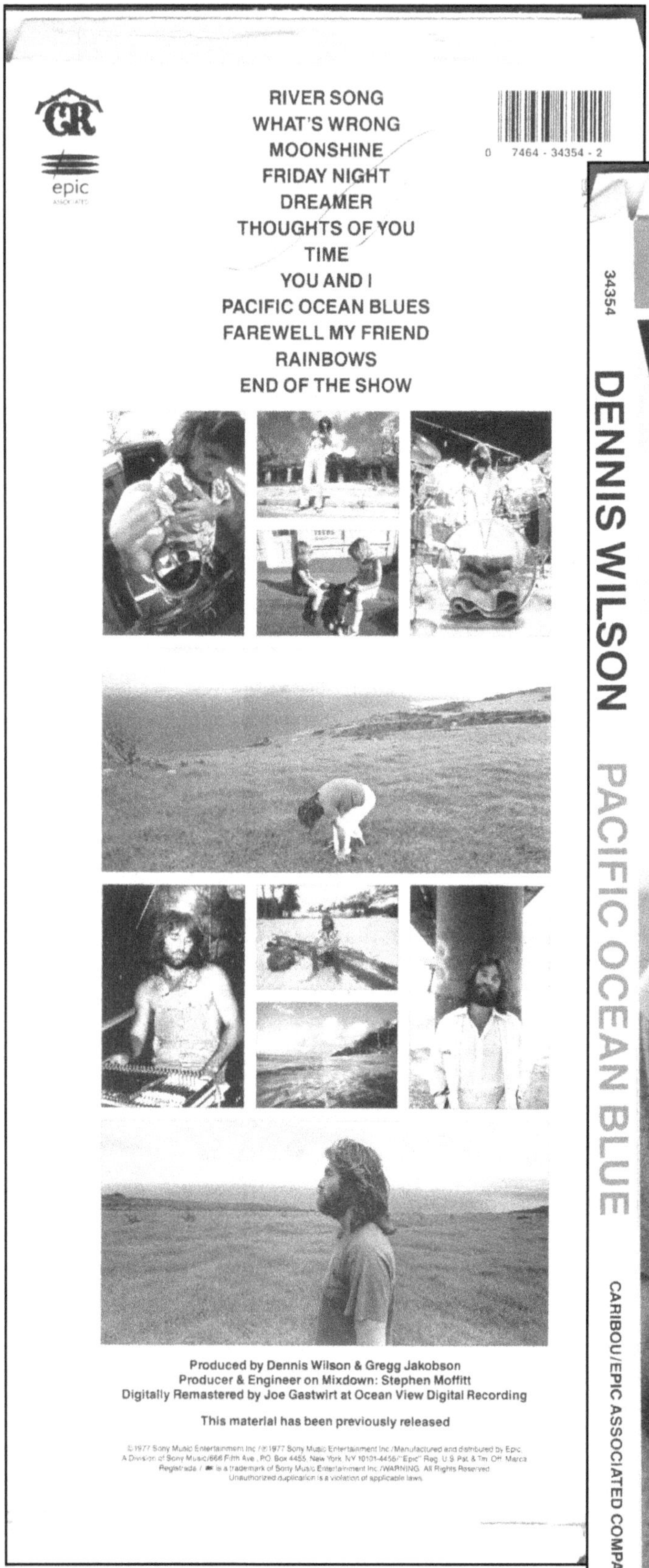

DENNIS WILSON - PACIFIC OCEAN BLUE

RIVER SONG
WHAT'S WRONG
MOONSHINE
FRIDAY NIGHT
DREAMER
THOUGHTS OF YOU
TIME
YOU AND I
PACIFIC OCEAN BLUES
FAREWELL MY FRIEND
RAINBOWS
END OF THE SHOW

0 7464-34354-2

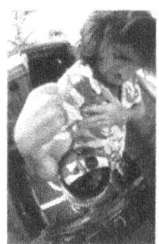

Produced by Dennis Wilson & Gregg Jakobson
Producer & Engineer on Mixdown: Stephen Moffitt
Digitally Remastered by Joe Gastwirt at Ocean View Digital Recording

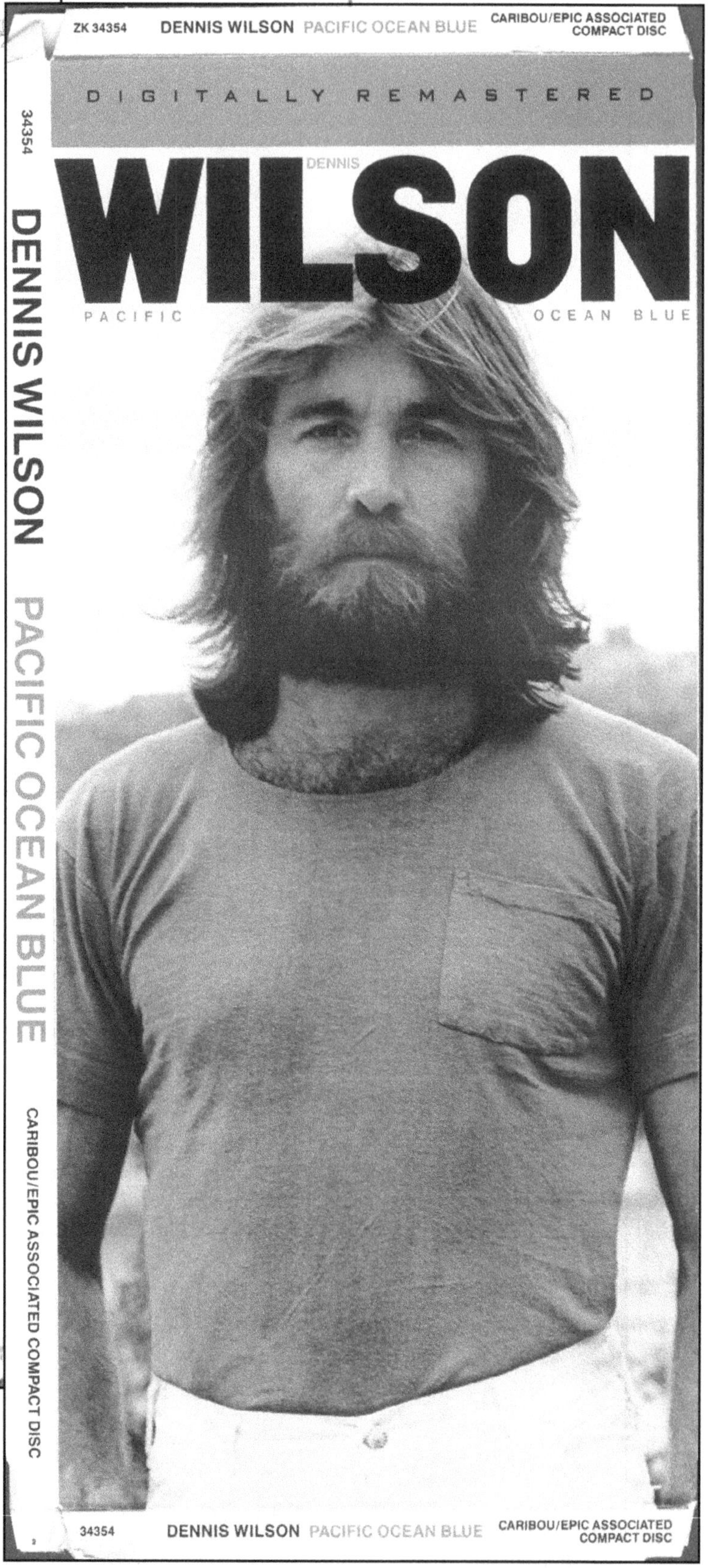

This material has been previously released

DENNIS WILSON

"Pacific Ocean Blue"—The first solo album by Dennis Wilson. Next week. On Caribou Records and Tapes.

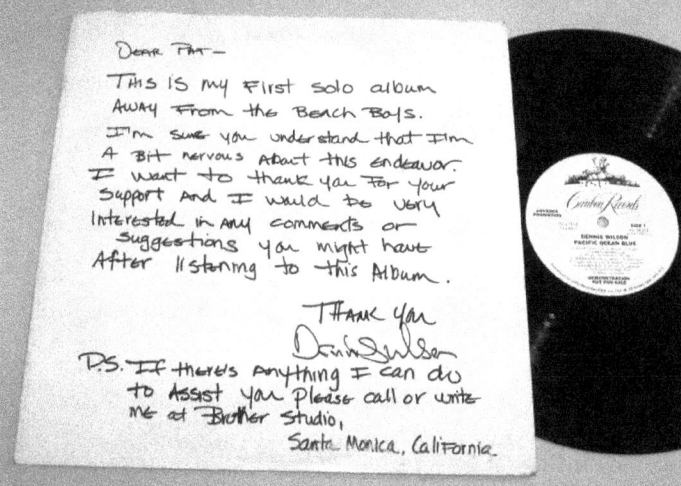

Dear Pat—
This is my first solo album away from the Beach Boys. I'm sure you understand that I'm a bit nervous about this endeavor. I want to thank you for your support and I would be very interested in any comments or suggestions you might have after listening to this Album.
Thank you
Dennis Wilson
P.S. If there's anything I can do to assist you please call or write me at Brother Studio, Santa Monica, California.

Pacific Ocean Blues
Dennis Wilson
Caribou (PZ 34354)
by Marie Sterner

It's finally happened: the first of the Beach Boys to make his debut as a solo artist. It's obvious that a lot of time and money were spent in an effort to showcase Dennis Wilson's material in the best way possible. There's only one flaw to be found on this album: it doesn't work. Actually it's technically perfect, but to the point that the songs themselves have become incidental to the studio wizardry.

Wilson's vocals are mercifully buried by that same production, but it becomes painfully apparent on the ballads that his voice is downright unmelodic and ragged, reminiscent of a less hoarse Tom Waits, while lacking Waits' impeccable poetry and sense of rhythm and timing.

The Beach Boys have never been known for their "meaningfull" lyrics, but they've managed to make the songs classics with their distinctive harmonic blend and catchy arrangements. Wilson takes that harmless banality to the outer limits with some of the most insipid lyrics ever to grace an inner sleeve. To add insult to injury, the track "Time" gets the award for Dumbest Lyrics on an Album, starts out as a pleasant, innocuous ballad, crescendos, literally out of nowhere and completely out of context with the basic "feel" of the song, to a full symphonic halt.

While most of the songs sound as if they're playing at the wrong speed (one of the biggest culprits being "Moonshine") there are a few bright moments when Wilson manages to do something both lyrically and musically. "Dreamer" and "Pacifc Ocean Blues" are the obvious standouts, as they manage to have somewhat less unispired lyrics than the other 10 tunes, and some genuinely funky lil' melodies. However, two good songs (and only relatively good songs at that) do not an album make. The album lacks any kind of style at all—we're never quite sure exactly what Wilson is trying to communicate. It sure doesn't sound like the Beach Boys, and if that was his intent, he succeeded. Problem is, it doesn't sound like much of anything else, either. Not much at all.

Raps

DENNIS WILSON

Photo by John Pinto

DENNIS WILSON

BEACHED BOY — A True Story — by GARY PIG

It was Monday, August 29, 1977, it was hot, and it was about to pour rain. But as always, it was a sunny Saturday afternoon inside Round Records, one flight high at 46 Bloor Street West in Toronto. Yet this was no ordinary Monday, coz Round was about to play host to another musical celebrity, and this time it wasn't some faded has-been direct from the Delete Zone or some semi-obscure suedo jazz reedist from a nearby supper club. No, this time it was to be one of the store's biggest catches ever: An authentic, direct-from-Malibu, Hawaiian-print-shirted, bronze-tanned, brazil-nut-toed Beach Boy. And no ordinary Beach Boy either: Not baby-chubby Carl, blissed-out Mike, snoozing Bri, or ex-dental student Al. Yes, Round Records was presenting Dennis Wilson, to some still the epitome of brainless brawn (remember beach movies?) but to others an artist who, via his just-released solo elpee PACIFIC OCEAN BLUE(S), is finally being allowed to have his say his way. You see, Den wasn't putting all his faith in his position as Beach Boy to sell his record, so he was spending his afternoons of this BB tour making the usual promotional rounds, and we found out.

Consequently (as always) PIG Was There: Johnny Pig was there, checking the settings on his prized camera one more time. Cindy Pig was there, paper and pen in hand, ready to record all goings-on. And yours truly was there, wondering whether or not I should ask Dennis about his top-secret associations with noted starlet butcher Charles "Never Learn Not To Love" Manson. The Beach Boys had played their first of two sell-out shows the night before at the Canadian National Exhibition, and all the reviews said "moreofthesamefromthecalifornianmogulsofsurfandsunwhocapturetheessenceofamericanyouthinasiablahh" and other such analytical pooh. (Nobody understands The Beach Boys but that's another story and another issue).

Larry Round, the man behind the scenes who fronts the Round Records empire, had donned cutoffs for the occasion, and Side Two of SURF'S UP rang over his store's P.A. Why weren't they playing Dennis' own album instead? Coz Columbia Records hadn't delivered it yet, of course. I hardly minded though: I'm always in the mood to sing along with "Till I Die".

The next thing we knew, it was nearing 2. The Beach Boy was late! Had he skipped ahead to CHUM-FM for his promised on-air blab session and forsaken Round's magnificent PACIFIC OCEAN BLUE wall display? We hoped not. Perhaps he was just out judging another beauty pageant, or removing his shirt for more publicity stills.

By 2:13 there was much worry one flight high at 46 Bloor Street West. The handful of semi-fans who'd gathered were beginning to drift out of the store, and wouldn't Dennis be upset if he wasn't to be mobbed affectionately as has been the case for most of his life. Larry anxiously darted between the phone and the window as the Pigs debated retiring to Harvey's for cheeseburgers with tomatoe only, please. SURF'S UP had run its course, and somebody was about to replace it with BEACH BABY by First Class: Oh God he'd better get here fast!

In the nick of time, preceeded by a gaggle of sun-glassed record biz heavies, Dennis Wilson mounted the stairs to Round Records, past the Simply Saucer posters, and into the store where he was greeted by a beaming Larry, full of Beach Boys anecdotes for the occasion. Along for the ride was Dennis' latest wife - the poised and peachy Karen. Together they made a handsome and duvely pair who'd be not one iota out of place at an industry cocktail bash or gulping boston cream pie aboard their luxury yacht.

The first thing I thought to myself as Denny walked by en route to rifle through the Beach Boys browser ("How's our new one doing Lar?") was "Christ, is he ever short!", but then the only rock star who's ever turned out to be as lengthly as I'd imagined a rock star should be was Ray(mond Douglas) Davies, and he likes disco shoes so maybe even he doesn't measure up. But what Dennis may have lacked in height he more than made up for horizontally: As Annette would say, "Boy, what a hunk!" No way was I gonna risk being thumped, so I scratched the Manson question out of my mind forever, and approached him from behind with my best

"Hi, Dennis!"

I outstretched my comparitively pale handshaker as my fellow Pigs moved in closer for support and pix. "I'm Gary of The PIG Paper, and I'd like to present you with a copy of our fifth issue, in which you'll note the words "The Beach Boys" on the cover and a review of THE BEACH BOYS LOVE YOU on Page 13". I shot this glorious run-on at him, and after he regained his composure, replied with his whitest promo smile, "Thank you". The interview was next.

THE DENNIS WILSON INTERVIEW
PIG: So your album's finally out. We've been waiting a long time for it.
DEN: I've got another one all ready. It should be out in January.
PIG: Great! By the way, we all love THE BEACH BOYS LOVE YOU.
DEN: Thanks very much.
PIG: When's the next Beach Boys album coming out?
DEN: Later this year. It's called ADULT CHILD.
PIG: Pardon?
DEN: ADULT CHILD.
PIG: Great! Was it recorded at the same time as the last one was?
DEN: A bit of it was, but most of it was recorded right after we finished the last one.
PIG: I heard you got the tapes of your album stolen when you were in Hawaii recently.
DEN: What? Oh that. That was just a cassette of the album.
PIG: Oh. Listen, There's one question I just have to ask you.
(PREDICTING THAT I HAD LOST MY MIND AGAIN AND WAS GOING TO STRIKE UP A CONVERSATION ABOUT CHARLES MANSON AFTER ALL, CINDY RETREATED AND JOHNNY PUT HIS LENS CAP ON. BUT INSTEAD:)

OCEAN

DENNIS WILSON

PIG: Whatever happened to David Marks?
DEN: I don't know, man. I have no idea.
(BUT WE FOUND OUT OURSELVES: READ PIG PAPER #7. SUDDENLY:)
DEN: Listen, I gotta go for a sec, so See you..... and, uhh, Thanks again.

And with that, he shot over to the budget bin (in search of copies of his oh so rare debut album I REMEMBER ENGLAND (Fiesta FLP-1232) no doubt), leaving me to have a perfectly nice little chat with Karen who seemed to have befriended me because I knew who she was without having to be introduced by her husband. She was busy acting the perfect rock'n'roll wife by tagging behind Dennis, shouting "Hey, Wilson!", and snapping shots of him. It was all getting just a touch too Rock Awards-ish for my taste, so after shoving a PIG poster at DW to autograph, Cindy and I split for our cheeseburger (bumping into no less than Elliot Gould on the way: What a star-studded afternoon!). We left Johnny behind, mumbling "Oh to be a rock star" as he took pictures of Karen taking pictures of Dennis and Larry.

That night, PIG braved the crush and went to the CNE to catch the final Beach Boys show. Opening act Ricci Martin, this year's Carl Wilson protoge and brother of ex-Dino, Desi And Billy bassist Dino Martin (both of whom are sons of Dean Martin) only made us more impatient for the headliners. (More Trivia: Billy Hinsche, also ex-DD&B, is now one of The Beach Boys' many road musicians as well as being Carl's brother in law. Don't you sometimes get the feeling all of L.A is in one way or another related to The BBs?) When Karen finally introduced them and "California Girls" began, the Exhibition Stadium went bonkers, swaying their glow-sticks to the beat and tossing beach balls to the sky. As is always the case, it was the mouldies from the Capitol Records catalog that were screamed at, and even Al Jardine dance steps and still more Mike Love wise-cracks ("...they have to take a boat because it's an island...") couldn't keep the throng interested in stuff like "Love Is A Woman", "All This Is That"(now THERE'S an obscure one!) or "Airplane", during which everyone applauded in the pre- "I can't wait to see her face" rest, thinking the song was over. Disgusting. Didn't any of you buy THE BEACH BOYS LOVE YOU? I thought I reviewed it so well in the last ish.....

The key to the show's success was It Was FUN. What more can be said? A lot of newavers and their fans could take a few lessons from The Beach Boys and their fans. And yes, "the musical sage of the age" Brian Wilson is STILL on the road with the band, and if the sound crew could've stayed awake maybe I could've heard him. He looked fairly slim, but I was too far away (without Rock Serling's trusty binocs) to see if he's really gotten a brush cut or not. Brian a punk rocker? Don't fool yourselves kids: He had short hair as early as '61.

Anyways, where was I? Oh yeh Dennis Wilson. Well, about a month after the concert I had Lagoona get a copy of PACIFIC OCEAN BLUE off Columbia for me: I was hesitant in laying out four or five $s for it retail and my precautions were correct. I don't think it's a very good album.

The cover is interesting: the word "Wilson" alone blares out at you, perhaps to trick the uninformed into thinking it's Brian or even Carl (would you believe Audree or yet another Capitol repackaging of THE MANY MOODS OF MURRY WILSON). Lotsa fab pix inside - no doubt the work of Karen imitating ace rival Linda

BLUE

DENNIS WILSON

McCartney's RAM layout. The inner sleeve drips Los Angeles session players'n'surf celebrities (contractual penguinheaps prevented fellow B.Boys from contributing vocally or instrumentally). But as we've all learned by now, beautiful design work and an all-star band does not necessarily spell "music", as I was about to discover upon dropping Side One on to the PIG Player.

"River Song" begins POB drearily enough. The annoying overproduction which stinks up this entire LP is at its worst here, though the snare work is admirable and the choir, of "That Same Song" fame, is worth hearing once. Ecology is the theme of the lyrics (I thought we all abandoned that crusade with SURF'S UP) and poor Carl, who should know better (though his involvement with a lemon like Ricci Martin makes me wonder), got stuck with half author's credit (blame?) along with Denny.

"What's Wrong" (good question), "Friday Night", and the title track are the closest this record comes to rockers. "What's Wrong" features a Brian Wilson piano riff with that SMILEY SMILE sound Eric "She Did It" Carmen is currently reaping a bundle with (everyone catches up with The Beach Boys sooner or later - usually later). "Friday Night" suffers from David Gilmour slide guitar and use of the words "white punks" (on dope?). Even Mike Love's TM mantra "mama-now-now-now" can't save "Pacific Ocean Blues". Where has the earotic rockin' Dennis of "All I Wanna Do" and "Got To Know The Woman" gone? I guess even Beach Boys get old.....

The remaining eight cuts mix shit with syrup: "Dreamer" could be the theme from an Afro-American teevee sitcom; "You And I" tries "She's Going Bald" percussion, "Farewell My Friend" B.Wilson finger-snatting, "Time" a C.Wilson up-tempo change, "Rainbows" A.Jardine banjo. None of these gimmicks work.

The only one of these silly love songs I'll ever play again is "Thoughts Of You", which is touchingly quaint despite the fact that Dennis the riff-off artist swiped a chord-change from the M*A*S*H theme. This cut states its sentiment sweetly and sparingly; most of POB's material must've begun life this way: If only DW could have spared them the Bacharachian shmultz. Co-author Jim Dutch must be responsible for lifting "Thoughts Of You" above the rest of these songs, but it isn't that great a piece really - it's not hard to out-shine the likes of "Moonshine" and "End Of The Show" which would've even been embarrassing along-side Dennis' CARL AND THE PASSIONS: SO TOUGH material. Maybe co-producer, chief co-writer Greg Jakobsen is to blame.....

Dennis! Remember "Forever", "Be Still", "Slip On Through" and other greats from your past? WHAT HAPPENED!?!

Right after their CNE concert, The Beach Boys had a big fight, and Dennis quit the band for a few days. Fortunately, he's back in the group now. Hopefully, that's where he'll stay, because PACIFIC OCEAN BLUE proves he's not ready for solosuperstardom. As for Brian, Carl, Mike and Al, I don't blame them for refusing to acknowledge Dennis' album: At least they can still smell dung.

No more fooling around, Boys: LOVE YOU and even 15 BIG ONES showed you can still do it, whether anyone realizes it or not. So I'm expecting revelations within ADULT CHILD, okay? Are you listening Boys?

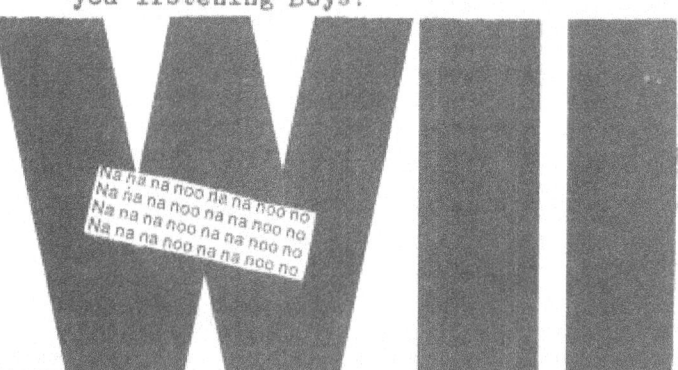

DENNIS WILSON

All Alone and On the Beach

Dennis Wilson's 'Pacific Ocean Blue' Is First Beach Boy Solo LP

by Scott Cohen

The Beach Boys began in the back seat of the Wilsons' family car one Friday night in 1961, when the three young brothers sang in three-part harmony. Later, brother Dennis turned to Brian and suggested that they sing a song about surfing—all the kids at school would love it. So Brian and cousin Mike Love wrote "Surfin'," and you know the rest.

Dennis—who rode a 9'2" surfboard—is the first Beach Boy in their sixteen year history to release a solo album. Nonetheless, the album, *Pacific Ocean Blue* (Brother), is not a surfing album. Nor do any of the Beach Boys appear on it, although his wife Karen Lamm, Billy Hinsche (he has sung backup vocals for years) and ex-Beach Boys Bruce Johnstone and Ricky Fataar, do.

Pacific Ocean Blue is, in fact, very un-Beach Boyish, if that's at all possible. Dennis—who flunked his army physical when he was caught with someone else peeing in his jar—always seemed a little different from the others.

The "meaning" of *Pacific Ocean Blue*, if an album could be said to have a "meaning," will not be found in any individual song, but in the impression the sum total of all the songs creates, just like it's not an individual snowflake, but the total accumulation of the storm—in Dennis' case, a sandstorm—that leaves an overall impression.

One gets the impression from listening to the album that his house is about to slip into the ocean, or a fist is about to come through the door. The punch itself, however, is felt, not in any one song, but in the spaces between them, just like the most moving parts of a great book are often read between the lines.

The tricky part of this album is that it sounds like so many others, although which, exactly, escapes us. This is not to say he is copying other people, or that *Pacific Ocean Blue* is, by comparison, inferior to them—rather, it's like playing with a good poker player who you feel has the winning card up his sleeve, but don't know which.

The quality of his voice resembles the quality of light as it mixes with the fog rolling off the sea. "The sunshine blinded me this morning love/ Like the sunshine, love comes and goes again . . ." in "Thoughts Of You," is sung in a sexy, gruff, late-at-night, another-cup-of-coffee, one-too-many-cigarettes sort of voice, to a wide awake one that's just had its first morning gulp of fresh sea air.

The hardest thing to identify is where the album's coming from—no doubt somewhere aloof, sexy and remote, like Dennis himself—and where it takes you. You don't know where, but it sends you there.

It's as if something in the date Dennis had been eating suddenly made him remember the tropics, just before an approaching storm. For him, the record was like having a short wave radio, one that could catch sounds coming from all directions. He had wanted the best album possible, just like he had wanted the best radio possible, as much so he could watch it spin on the turntable as to listen to it. Once a little deuce coupe had been his joy-thought. Now, when Dennis wheels through the California night, he can think of his record spinning out in the future, forever uniting himself with his listeners, no matter how distant they may be, whether in Japan, Java or the twenty-first century.

Dennis Wilson was the inspiration for "Surfin'." He still rides the California waves avidly.

CIRCUS MAGAZINE/25

DENNIS WILSON

Fleetwood Mac's Christine McVie & Beach Boy's Dennis Wilson visit KHJ Studios. Pictured left to right: McVie, KHJ's Bobby Ocean, Wilson, & KHJ's Program Director Chuck Martin.

Brother Dennis Branches Out

by Matt Stump

Normally, when a drummer goes solo, no one bats an eyelash. Why should they, when the focus on drummers in the majority of rock bands is minor? How can their solo work be at all interesting? It depends on how versatile they are musically and if their big brother is Brian Wilson. Such is the case with Dennis Wilson and his recent solo effort, "Pacific Ocean Blue" the first such undertaking of an original Beach Boy.

The album is a hodgepodge of differing styles and tempos. There is lots of rhythm, some blues, some gospel, some rock and roll, some mellow love songs, and a few classic harmonies familiar to anyone who ever went to the beach. The number of backup musicians, vocalists, and technicians is staggering.

No matter how pretty Dennis may be, his voice does not match. It is best suited to the rock and roll cuts. Those cuts are obvious both musically and lyrically because they contain the words, "rock and roll." Although you may find yourself tapping to "What's Wrong" it is such a weak novelty song that it should be the first to get scratched. A real Ringo Starr effort if there ever was one.

The addition of many and varied instruments (Wilson plays over 6 himself on the album including clarinet, violin, piano, drums, oboe, moog) and a dozen background vocalists, not to mention the Double Rock Baptist Choir, serve not only to enhance the music which they do well, but to save such love songs as "Moonshine" and "Thoughts of You" from Dennis' straining voice. Things are touchy until the sopranos, basses and synthesizers come in to save the day. Clearly without help, he can't handle the ballads. This background produces an anthemlike effect which saves the song.

The title cut, "Pacific Ocean Blue" and "Dreamer" are both funky and bluesy. "Pacific Ocean Blue" even carries environmental overtones about whales, otters and pollution, rarely approached lyrically, especcially by a Beach Boy.

"Dreamer" has got the biggest brass track on the album and usually the big classical backing to Wilson's tunes make the difference, yet for some strange reason we get a tuba in there. Even experimentation has its limits.

The second side is the stronger of the two by virtue of some sorely needed guitar work and Dennis' piano plinkings. The best track on the side is "Rainbows." Wilson's catchy piano work and someone's sweet Spanish guitar work make this track what it is, not earthshaking, merely pleasant. The problem of the album remains and is acute to over half the songs — they end too soon. The three minute mold is glaringly apparent in this work and an unfortunate occurrence because the foundation for good lyric and musical passages is there if it would only be expanded on. He had enough time, help and tutelage, to presumably produce FM style work but at least he delivered us from boring drum solos, his voice, and the disco craze, common fallacies these days. We have been waiting ten years to see if anything big and different would come from these boys, and if much attention is focused on Brian and his recovery, others may be overlooked. Let us not overlook Dennis Wilson but not look too long until we really have a fully expanded, unique work, one which avoids the trappings of novelty and disco and leaves the Beach Boy sound to history, not to be revived commercially summer after summer.

Beach Boy Dennis Wilson, whose first solo album, "Pacific Ocean Blue," is a step in the right direction, anyway. "Let us not overlook Dennis Wilson, but not look too long..."

DENNIS WILSON

Beach Boy's Death Is Investigated

LOS ANGELES (AP) — The alcohol level in Beach Boys drummer Dennis Wilson's blood when he drowned was 2½ times the legal limit for California drivers, possibly giving him a sense of "bravado" before he dove into cold water, a doctor says.

Toxicological tests found Wilson had a 0.26 percent blood-alcohol level at the time of his Dec. 28 death, coroner's spokesman Bill Gold said Friday. He refused to say whether the alcohol contributed to Wilson's death, which the coroner's office previously classified as an accidental drowning.

But a physician who briefly worked with the 39-year-old musician in an alcohol treatment program said, "It's not at all unfair to say the alcohol contributed to the accident."

Dr. Joe Takamine, of the chemical dependency unit at St. John's Hospital in Santa Monica, said, "He did have a problem with alcohol and that is going to influence how you react." Wilson quit the program after two days and drowned three days later.

Wilson died while diving for scrap in 58-degree water off a friend's boat in a slip at Marina del Rey.

Beach Boy's death ruled accidental

LOS ANGELES (AP) — Beach Boys drummer Dennis Wilson, mourned by the president and show business colleagues as a musician "everybody loved," drowned accidentally while diving, a coroner has ruled.

President Reagan was among those expressing sorrow Thursday over the death of Wilson, 39, who was pulled from 13 feet of water where he had been diving from a boat slip in suburban Marina del Rey.

During the autopsy Thursday, Deputy Medical Examiner J.L. Cogan found a "minor" abrasion on the Wilson's head, said Los Angeles County Coroner's spokesman Bill Gold. But he said that injury was "not in itself significant for a cause of death."

"The musician's death was listed as accidental," Gold said.

A sheriff's deputy said Wilson had been drinking with friends Wednesday on the 52-foot yawl Emerald before he began diving into a vacant slip.

Routine tests to detect alcohol or drugs in Wilson's body will take days or possibly weeks, Gold said.

Reagan and his wife, Nancy, became defenders of the Beach Boys last summer when then-Secretary of the Interior James Watt banned them from a July 4 performance on the Washington Mall.

After the incident, Mrs. Reagan invited the band to perform at the White House.

The Reagans, vacationing in Southern California, were "shocked and deeply saddened to learn of Dennis Wilson's death," said Mark Weinberg, an assistant White House press secretary.

"He was so vibrant and gifted, lovable," said Elliott Lott, the band's road manager. "He was a very sensitiybody loved him."

Probe Continues In Beach Boy's Death

LOS ANGELES (UPI) — It will take at least a week to determine if alcohol or drugs contributed to the accidental drowning of Beach Boys drummer Dennis Wilson, the coroner's office said after an autopsy.

"The death is listed as accidental drowning," coroner's spokesman Bill Gold said Thursday, adding it will take a week to determine the alcohol content in his blood and several weeks to detect whether he had taken any drugs. The tests are routine.

Funeral plans were incomplete, but Beach Boys spokesman Sandy Friedman said the family planned to meet today to discuss burial details.

Friedman said the surviving group members would "go on tour as planned" starting Jan. 24 in Troy, Ala., with concerts also planned in Texas, Louisiana, Colorado, South Dakota and Lake Tahoe on the California-Nevada border.

Wilson, 39, drowned Wednesday afternoon while diving "for old chairs and junk" from a boat slip at Marina del Rey. Investigators said he had been drinking for several hours with friends on a sailboat before he dived into the 58-
(Cont'd on Page 2)

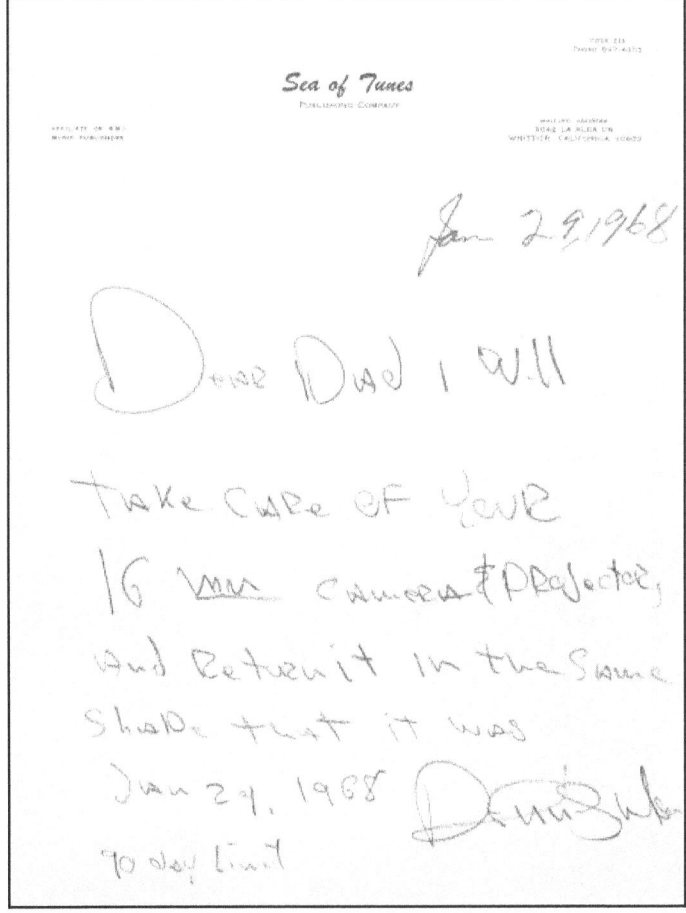

BECKLEY-LAMM-WILSON

Henry Diltz

" 'Til the beat begins
'Til the voices blend ...

The tide rolls in
Wait for your wave, there'll be another
And we will sing
I love you still like a brother."*

Gerry Beckley of **America**
Robert Lamm of **Chicago**
and
Carl Wilson of **The Beach Boys**

An emotional, spiritual song cycle of unforgettable melodic and lyrical strength.

Available everywhere June 20, 2000

*Lyrics by Carl Wilson and Phil Galdston
©2000, Murry Gage (ASCAP)/Kazzoom Music, Inc. (ASCAP)

You can always find out more at **www.transparentmusic.com**.

SUNRAYS

THE SUN RAYS are America's newest group sensation. Their "Follow The Sun" has become one of the big hits of 1965.

THE SUNRAYS
("Don't Take Yourself Too Seriously")

THE SUNRAYS
JOIN THE GALAXY OF STARS APPEARING IN

THE BEACH BOYS SUMMER SPECTACULAR

COW PALACE
SAN FRANCISCO
FRIDAY, JUNE 24th
8 P.M.

HOLLYWOOD BOWL
LOS ANGELES
SATURDAY, JUNE 25th
8 P.M.

SUNRAYS

Sunrays at KRLA

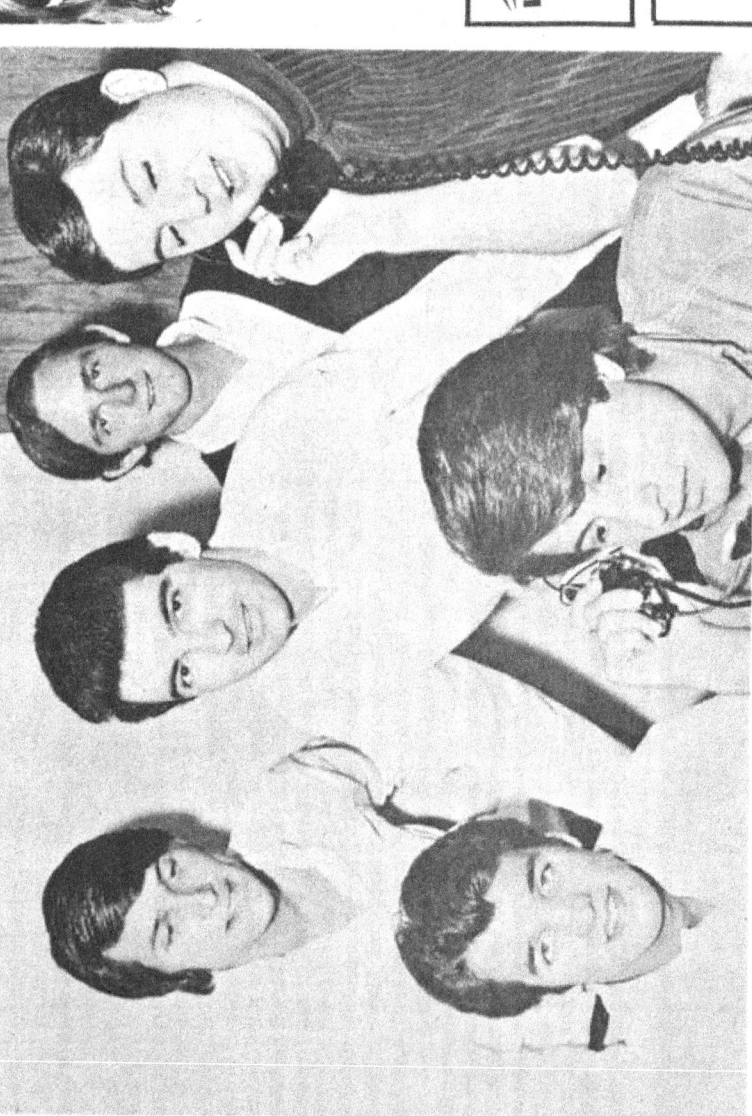

VINCE HOZIER AND BYRON CASE chat with fans in the lobby.

Drum City – Guitar Town
15255 Sherman Way, Van Nuys
5611 Jumilla, Woodland Hills
6226 Santa Monica Blvd. L.A.

2 free "Crazy Fill" book covers. $5 gift certificate with $15 one-time or accumulated purchase. Member's friends may purchase on his accumulation.
USE YOUR FUNTEEN BONUS COUPON "D"

The One And Only
BO DIDDLEY
July 12-24

THE SUNRAYS dropped by KRLA to answer the request lines and found DJ Johnny Hayes all willing to help.

BEAT Photos: Ron Donell

SUNRAYS

BO DIDDLEY
And His Chicago Blues Band
Originators of the Big Beat

AT DOUG WESTON'S

Troubadour

9083 SANTA MONICA BLVD.
L.A. NEAR DOHENY

RESERVATIONS
CR 6-6168

Join the "In" Crowd!

Brave New World

(The Club where LOVE first started)

The wildest dance club in Hollywood! Hollywood's only private club for top and upcoming recording groups, dancers, talent scouts and those with a musical interest. And their firends.

We are considering applications for a limited time only.

The BRAVE NEW WORLD features dancing to live entertainment 10 p.m. to 2 a.m., starring the best of Hollywood's rock and roll groups.

Membership applications must include name, address, age (18 over only), musical interest or group and agency name, personal reference and a $3 membership fee.

Mail to the BRAVE NEW WORLD

1642 No. Cherokee Ave.
Hollywood, California

Private Parties Are Also Arranged — *Call 462-9826*

Now A New Funteen Sponsor! Hobby-Land
HOBBY SHOP
1528 S. Robertson Blvd.
Let's Get Acquainted
Come In and See Our Complete Selection Of
Handicraft Supplies: Plastic resins, crystals, paper mache, etc. Model Kits Autos, planes, boats, animals, etc.
Phone 838-5802
Open weekdays 'til 7, Sat. til 3 p.m.

Use your Funteen Coupon "K"
Kookie Kapers
$5 certificate with $15 purchase
OL 4-9161   7860 Santa Monica Bl.
Store Hours 10-6:30 — Mon-Fri. 9 p.m.
Hosiery — Sportswear — Lingerie

A WORLD ON WHEELS
Antiques, Classics, Sportscars, Custom and Experimental, Hotrods, Motorcycles and Competition Machines.
6 Great Shows in One
Sun. — Aug. 7 — Rose Bowl
8 A.M. 'til 5 P.M.

EVEN CASEY KASEM stopped in for a few minutes to thank the guys for helping out with the many calls.

SUNRAY MARTI DI GIOVANNI signs a few autographs on his way out.

SUNRAYS

Rock On The Road

SUNRAYS
AUGUST
15-18 — Tour Canada with Beach Boys
19 — Spokane, Washington
20 — Tour with Raiders

TURTLES
AUGUST
19-24 — Miami Beach, Fla.
25 — Baltimore, Maryland
27 — Society party in San Francisco
29-31 — Tape Hollywood Palace

GARY LEWIS
AUGUST
18-20 — Elmira, New York
21-27 — Steel Pier, Atlantic City
30-31 — Detroit, Michigan State Fair

PETULA CLARK
AUGUST 1-JANUARY 15
In the U.S. for TV shows and 30 concerts.

KNICKERBOCKERS
AUGUST
17-27 — Seattle, Washington

PAUL REVERE & THE RAIDERS
AUGUST
20 — Asbury Park, New Jersey
21 — Wallingford, Conn.
22 — Manchester, New Hampshire
23 — Holyoke, Mass.
24 — Cleveland, Ohio
25 — Baltimore, Maryland
26 — Jacksonville, Fla.
27 — Tampa, Fla.
28 — Orlando, Fla.
29 — Miami Beach, Fla.
30 — Lafayette, La.
31 — Omaha, Neb.

EVERLY BROTHERS
AUGUST
15-21 — Deerborn, Michigan
23 — Plainview, Texas
24 — Clovis, New Mexico
25 — Lubbock, Texas
26 — Odessa, Texas
27 — Amarillo, Texas

LOVE
AUGUST
18 — Fresno, California
27 — Longshoremans, San Francisco

P.J. PROBY
SEPTEMBER
14-28 — Tour in Australia

JOHNNY RIVERS
AUGUST
13-27 — Army Reserves

LOVIN' SPOONFUL
AUGUST
24 — Connecticut
27 — Ohio
28 — Ohio
31 — Michigan
SEPTEMBER
5-18 — Vacation

CYRKLE
AUGUST
12-29 — Beatle tour
31 — Phoenix
SEPTEMBER
3 — Ohio
4 — Illinois

ROY HEAD
AUGUST
21-28 — Regal Theater, Chicago

LEAVES
SEPTEMBER
2- 8 — Miami, Fla.

THEM
AUGUST
16-21 — Losers North. San Jose, California
23-28 — Same
SEPTEMBER
2- 3 — Longshoreman's, San Francisco
9 — Fresno, California

VOGUES
AUGUST
20 — Chicago, Ill.
26 — Illinois
30 to Sept. 4 — Texas tour

JERRY NAYLOR
AUGUST
21 — State Fair in Wisconsin

MITCH RYDER AND THE DETROIT WHEELS
AUGUST
19-28 — "Where the Action Is" — Dick Clark Tour
19 — Commack, Long Island
20 — Hershey, Pa.
21 — Cleveland, Ohio
22 — Johnstown, Pa.
23 — Ithaca, New York
24 — Providence, Rhode Island
25 — Worchester, Mass.
26 — Long Beach, L.I., N.Y.
27 — Newburg, Pa.
28 — Evansburg, Pa.

ANIMALS
AUGUST
17-23 — New York City, N.Y.
24 — Phoenix, Arizona
25 — Manatu Beach, Michigan
26 — Harbor Springs, Michigan
27 — Midland, Michigan
28 — Benton Harbor, Michigan
29 — Mendon, Mass.
30-Sept. 5 — Steel Pier, New Jersey (Atlantic City)
SEPTEMBER
5 — Return to England

YARDBIRDS
AUGUST
18 — Tulsa, Oklahoma
19-20 — Oklahoma City, Okla.
21 — Tucson, Arizona
22 — Los Angeles, California
23 — Avalon, Catalina Island
24 — Monterey, California
25 — San Francisco, California
26 — San Leandro, California
27 — Santa Barbara, California
28 — Pismo Beach, California
29 — San Diego, California
30 — San Jose, California
SEPTEMBER
1 — Santa Rosa, California
3 — Salem, Oregon
4 — Honolulu, Hawaii

BEAU BRUMMELS
AUGUST
14-31 — VACATION
SEPTEMBER
2 — Hastings, Nebraska
3 — Green Bay, Wisconsin
4 — Medina, Ohio
6 — Lima, Ohio
7 — Visalia, California
24 — Springfield, Virginia

SUNRAYS

GROOVY NEW GROUPS

THE SUNRAYS

Each weekend you will find many Southern California students cruising along Hollywood Blvd. and the Strip looking for the action. Among these people you will find the SUNRAYS. Five groovy guys with great sounds. Their first hit record "I Live For The Sun" caused quite a stir and the boy's knew they couldn't be satisfied with one hit. So the start of a great new group began. Blue eyed Rick Henn, is probably the kookiest one of the group. Rick plays drums and also wrote and sang lead on the Sunrays two biggest hits. Just follow a guitar and you will find Byron Case. Byron is the quietest and one of the nicest Sunrays. Next is 6'3" blue eyed Vince Hozier. All the Sunrays concerts are emceed by Vince. He also plays bass guitar. And now the lady killer of the group, lead guitarist Eddie Medora. Born in Chicago, home to Eddie is California. The speaker for the house is Marty DiGiovanni. Marty also plays electric organ and piano. After hearing them sing you can be sure the Sunrays will be around for many a sunset.

SUNRAYS

Sunrays: 'It Takes A Lot Of Capital'

The Sunrays are not the Beach Boys. They are not related to the Beach Boys and they don't intentionally mean to sound like them. It *is* true, however, that the Sunrays once wore the same striped shirts which have become the Beach Boys' trademark, and it's also true that Murray Wilson (Beach Boys Carl, Brian and Dennis' father) is their manager.

Whether their association with the Beach Boys has been a help or a hinderance to the Sunrays depends on which side of the fence you're peering over. From what they themselves say, one gets the definite impression that the Sunrays are not the least bit worried about it and rather tend to think that it has helped their career along.

However, they become quite uptight if confronted by publicity claiming that they are a mere imitation of the Beach Boys. "We didn't try to follow them," admitted Eddie, "it's just natural. When you sing five part harmony it always comes out that way."

They joke and kid around about Murray Wilson but they really think the world of him and state frankly that if it wasn't for him they would probably still be playing local clubs and school dances.

"He's the greatest man in the whole world and if he told me to jump out of the window — I wouldn't," laughed Rick.

"The thing that nobody realizes is that it takes a lot of capital to get a group started," said Marty. "Our manager is interested in us not only as dollar signs but he's like a father to us and he took a great risk in us."

That risk has apparently paid off as the Sunrays have had two giant smashes—"I Live For The Sun" and "Andrea." And "Still," their latest release, is making noise in certain parts of the country and from the way it's selling, looks as if it will break out all over the nation.

The Sunrays are all in college and find that mixing school with a career is "very hard." They manage by appearing on weekends, touring during vacations and studying in between.

For instance, Easter vacation found them in such places as Portland, Salt Lake City, Vancouver and Toronto, and this summer the Sunrays head out on a 60 day cross country tour which will hit practically every major city in the nation.

Switching the talk from strictly Sunrays to general competition in the pop field today we wondered if the Sunrays found themselves faced with more competition than when they began playing five years ago.

"It's always been competitive," answered Rick. "The span of a hit record now is so short, which is why there are more groups around today."

The Sunrays are probably one of the most outspoken groups on the scene — they know what they like, dislike and feel strongly about. "We don't dig people who come on too strong," declared Rick, "you know, people who've had one hit record and come on strong. We're the humbliest guys in the world!"

They also don't like artists who come out with the same sounding records time after time. "We don't like that at all," said Byron. "It's bad and in poor taste."

"It's like saying to the kids that they're a bunch of idiots. A bad record will never make it," finished up Vince.

"It's like Motown," said Marty re-opening the closed subject. "I'm really getting sick of Motown, every record sounds the same. But they keep selling — wow!"

It's been quite a while since I've heard an artist say that they really dug Elvis but that's exactly what Byron told me. In fact, he even has a horse named Elvis. "Elvis has always been one of my biggest fans," said Byron howling when he discovered that he had just said it backwards. "Seriously, I've always dug that cat. This horse reminded me of him."

And with that the Sunrays proceeded to sing "Still" at the top of their five ample voices, devour all *The BEAT's* in the office and then proceed merrily down the hall and out of the building. Too much — that's all we can say!

...THE SUNRAYS IN THEIR OLD STRIPED SHIRTS AND WHITE PANTS.

Wilson To Wax Album

Murray Wilson, the father of Beach Boys, Brian, Dennis and Carl Wilson, has been signed by Capitol Records as one of the company's first independent producers.

Wilson, who was the Beach Boys' personal manager in its beginning years, can be credited with a good deal of their initial success. Wilson's new album will be a collection of songs penned by Don Ralke, Eck Kinor and Rick Helm of the Sunrays, as well as by Wilson himself.

THE MODERN SUNRAYS (top to bottom, Marty DiGiovanni, Eddie Medora, Rick Henn, Byron Case and Vince Hozier) in their up-dated, modern velours.

SUNRAYS

...**FINALLY** on stage the five Sunrays (l. to r. Marty, Byron, Eddie, Rick and Vince) introduce their latest disc, "Don't Take Yourself Too Seriously."

Behind The Curtains At A Sunrays' Concert

You file in and take your seat in the auditorium. You glance around, size up the rest of the audience and settle back for waht you hope will be a short wait until the show gets underway. And usually without warning, it happens. The curtains part, the MC steps to the mike and the show which you have shelled out three of four dollars to see finally begins.

If you're lucky, everything runs smoothly. There are no huge hang-ups, the performers head out one after the other, mass confusion and obvious goofs are missing. You watch, you laugh, you scream, you cry. Or maybe you just sit there and applaude.

And then as suddenly as it had begun – it's over. For minutes, perhaps only for seconds, you sit perfectly still hoping that your favorite will re-appear. When he doesn't, you slowly wander out of the auditorium and pile into your car, linger at ths bus stop, or wait for your family car to pull into sight.

Through the entire ordeal you have found your mind being constantly plagued with the re-occuring question: "What's going on backstage." What IS happening behind those curtains which separate you from him?

To find out, we enlisted the aid of the five Sunrays and being extremely helpful guys they invited *The BEAT* and hired their OWN photographers to snap shots of exactly what went on backstage at one of their college dates.

Actually, the Sunrays were naturals for this kind of a feature as they spend a good deal of their time playing "live" dates and while they admit frankly that nothing can beat the excitement of a concert, they are quick to reveal that it's not ALL fun and games.

There is a tremendous amount of work involved, long hours of rehearsal, the loading and the unloading of instruments and a million small (but vitally important) details which must be worked out.

To the Sunrays, each concert is a new challenge but a challenge which they are eager to accept. Their hard work has paid off well for them because they are now known as "crowd pleasers." And quite honestly, they are. They enjoy performing and this becomes immediately obvious to their audiences, making for a harmonious feeling throughout the whole auditorium.

So, thanks to the Sunrays the next time you attend a concert you won't wonder what your favorites are doing – you'll know.

...**EDDIE** chats with **The BEAT** before leaving.

...**BYRON**, Marty and Rick take down the equipment which they had set up less than two hours before.

SUNRAYS

Sunrays at KRLA

THE SUNRAYS dropped by KRLA to answer the request lines and found DJ Johnny Hayes all willing to help.

VINCE HOZIER AND BYRON CASE chat with fans in the lobby.

EVEN CASEY KASEM stopped in for a few minutes to thank the guys for helping out with the many calls.

SUNRAY MARTI DI GIOVANNI signs a few autographs on his way out.

HONEYS

 RHINO RECORDS JUNE 1983 RELEASE

THE HONEYS

RNLP 851 $8.98 List

The Honeys have been known throughout the 1970's for their close association with the Beach Boys. They are led by Marilyn Wilson (Brian's wife), and in the past were always produced by Brian (under the name "American Spring"). This exciting package showcases a contemporary hard pop approach akin to Pat Benatar and two previously unrecorded Brian Wilson songs are included.

The best recordings by America's premier 1960's punk band, including all of their chart hits, such as "Dirty Water," "Sometimes Good Guys Don't Wear White," "Try It," and several rare tracks.

THE BEST OF THE STANDELLS

RNLP 107 $8.98 List

The first album in print in almost thirteen years by the band who has long been considered America's most famous acid rock group. This comprehensive collection features their best songs, as well as rare singles and a previously unreleased track.

THE BEST OF THE CHOCOLATE WATCHBAND

RNLP 108 $8.98 List

THE BEST OF SLIM HARPO

RNLP 106 $8.98 List

This compilation is the first to feature all the hits by the singularly most important Blues influence of the 1960's. The songs included are "Shake Your Hips" and "I'm A King Bee" (recorded by the Rolling Stones), "Got Love If You Want It" (recorded by the Who and the Kinks, as well as Harpo's own top ten hit, "Baby, Scratch My Back". A must for Blues and Rock fans alike.

JERRY LEE LEWIS GREATEST HITS

RNDF 255 $8.98 List

The heppest picture disc ever set to wax, Jerry Lee's greatest and most memorable Sun Records hits are presented here, including "Great Balls of Fire," "Whole Lotta Shakin' Goin' On," and "High School Confidential".

This LP represents Rhino's continued efforts to reissue important rare recordings of the sixties. One of the few live shows of this era to be recorded, the artists in attendance are a who's who of early sixties rock n' roll, including Freddie Cannon, The Righteous Brothers, Jan & Dean, The Ronettes, etc. In addition, the orchestra for the show is conducted by the legendary Phil Spector.

MEMORIES OF THE COW PALACE

RNLP 105 $8.98 List

HONEYS PROMO PHOTO 1983 with LIVE SIGNATURES

SPRING

SHYIN' AWAY
(Sandler-Rovell-Wilson)
AMERICAN SPRING
Produced by Brian Wilson
& David Sandler
Columbia   Time 2:54
Flip — "Falling In Love"

Ben Edmonds knows what we'll wake up to around this time next year; Spring. Last year his reviews and notices called the nation's attention to these girls' first album, which was on UA. Since that time they've shifted headquarters to Columbia, the ancestral home of surf and California consciousness. After all it was Columbia who first introduced Bruce Johnston through SURFIN ALL AROUND THE WORLD. And the Rip Choros, Bruce and Terry and Jan & Dean's latter recordings for the label were no jerk-offs either. Besides everything, we're quite prepared for Spring. And they're real girls too, with all the fixin's — permanently, none of that weekend stuff...full time chicks. And brother, it's about time. What a relief.

Yep, the backlash has arrived. Time for the right-wing to check in and ya know the beach, drive-in hamburger joints (see Robot Hull's definitive account of such essentials in the March issue of CREEM) and tits aren't that bad after all. And Spring sing about all that kind of natural stuff. Going steady. Making out. Backing off. Prick teasing.

I'm shyin' away from you, shyin' away from feeling blue/
Yes I know what I want and I really don't want to/
Yes I know what I want and I really can't let you.*

Leave it to Brian Wilson to deliver us from the transsexual evils of 1973. Those who've paid attention these past twelve months know all about Brian's main interests on record for the last two years...of course it's been Spring. Spring are Diane Rovell and Marilyn Wilson. They're sisters and Marilyn is Brian's wife. They used to be called the Honeys and recorded the classic 1963 non-hit *Surfin' Down the Swannee River.* Extremely important.

Now summer is approachin', and aside from Dean Torrence's *Legendary Masked Surfers*, Bruce Johnston's and Terry Melcher's *California*, Rick Henn (former leader of the Sunrays), Spring will be among the top surf music revivalists when that scene makes it once again. Spring are to Surf music what Gerry & The Pacemakers, Peter & Gordon, and Ian Whitcomb were to the Beatle movement.

*©1973 Brother Music

It's Spring again, just in time for summer. Brian Wilson does it again, along with wife Marilyn and Diane Rovell. Honeys revisited.

SPRING

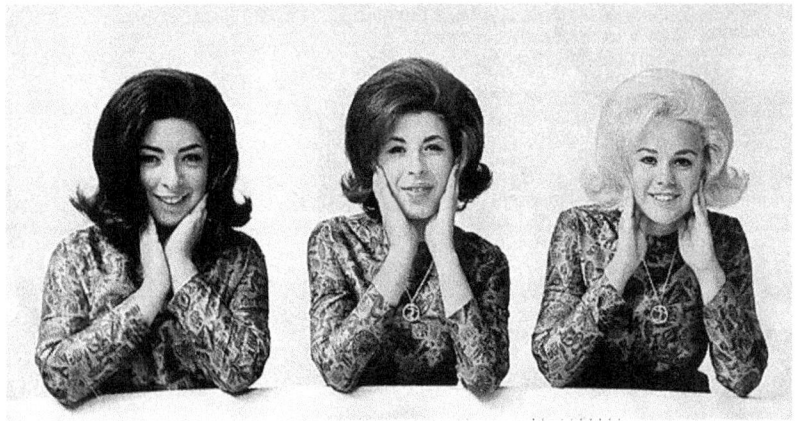

SPRING

SPRING

SPRING
(WITH BRIAN WILSON)

CAPTAIN AND TENNILLE

The Captain and Tennille Believe in Togetherness

By DICK KLEINER

HOLLYWOOD (NEA) — "Love Will Keep Us Together," sang The Captain and Tennille. On the strength of that one hit record, they got themselves a TV show.

But the song did more than make them rich and famous. It could be considered their national anthem. Because they claim that love will, indeed, keep them together.

They share everything, at this loving moment in their lives. They share philosophy, fortune and fads. They shared a way of life, they share work, they share play. In fact, they are somewhat old-fashioned in their outlook on sharing.

Toni Tennille is a beauty, and it's easy to imagine her as a leading lady in motion pictures. But she says no, she won't do it, at least not if the film would include a love scene with her leading man.

"I'd never act in a movie," Toni says, "If there was a love scene with somebody else. I just have a feeling that that wouldn't be right, because Daryl is the only man for me."

Unlike some couples, they don't seem to feel the urge for privacy. They say that they haven't been apart for more than 11 hours since they began living together, four years ago.

They even have the same attitude toward the question of children.

"We have no plans to have any children," says Daryl Dragon, then turning the floor over to Toni, as usual, for a more detailed explanation.

"We feel strongly," she says, "that the only reason to bring children into the world would be if you thought they might make a contribution to humanity. And you just can't

DARYL DRAGON AND TONI TENNILLE

be sure if your own children would make such a contribution."

So they are childless, but not children-less. Toni has three sisters and Daryl has two brothers and two sisters. Among their seven siblings, they have a flock of nieces and nephews.

Uncle Daryl and Aunt Toni dote on their nieces and nephews. Tony says the kids love Daryl.

"He's wonderful with kids," she says. "He's a very funny man and he does little pantomime routines for them. He used to do them for me and that's one reason I fell in love with him. He does one in which he eats a bunch of bananas while he's hiding behind a post."

Toni and Daryl met in San Francisco. There is some similarity to their paths which brought them here.

Daryl Dragon is the son of Carmen Dragon, a famous conductor of symphonic music. He started Daryl out on the piano when he was three.

"That was too young," he says. "I had no interest in it then. But I came back to it later."

He worked with several groups, until he found his niche as the keyboard player with The Beach Boys. He was with that noted group for several years.

Meanwhile, down in Montgomery, Ala., Toni Tennille was growing up. Her father, Frank Tennille, had been a singer — with Ben Pollack and Bob Crosby — until he left the music business to take over the family furniture business in Montgomery.

She studied classical piano and voice (later dancing, too) and she did some acting. Then she, too, joined a group. They were in San Francisco when they needed a new keyboard player.

Dragon, then at loose ends, went up to San Francisco and fit right in.

"I knew right away," says Toni, "that he was going to mean something to me. I get strong feelings about people and they're usually accurate."

They began living together in 1972, and the union was legalized in 1974. By that time, they had decided to form their own group, The Captain and Tennille.

His nickname — The Captain — was given to him by one of The Beach Boys. It was a natural nickname, because he had long worn yachting caps.

The hats and the nickname really have nothing to do with the sea. Daryl says he's always liked boats but has never had one. Now, when he could easily afford one, he doesn't have the time to indulge a hobby.

Toni was always tall as a child and now is a statuesque 5'11". She says that, as an adolescent, her height bothered her. She used to stoop a little, to try and minimize her stature.

"And then a memorable thing happened," she says. "When I was 13, I was confirmed and the bishop was present. He commented on my being very tall and then he said, 'Someday, you'll love being tall. You should stand up straight and be proud of your height.' Since then, I have."

TALK

BY CHARLES H. GOREN AND OMAR SHARIF

had passed originally. However, his flat hand and the fact that he held only three-card support caused him to adopt a more leisurely approach. But when South jump rebid his own suit, North had something in reserve for his raise to game.

West led a diamond and, when dummy appeared, declarer could see nine tricks. He realized that a tenth would materialize if either West held the king of diamonds or East the ace of hearts. Looking no further, declarer tried the diamond finesse. This lost and East shifted to a heart. Declarer put up the king, but West topped it and the defenders took two more heart tricks to set the contract.

Declarer could count himself unlucky in that he had about a 3 to 1 chance to land his game. We judge him more sternly. His heart holding should have alerted him to the fact that he could ill afford to let East gain the lead, and his efforts should have been directed to keeping the dangerous defender off play.

Correct technique is to win the first trick with the ace of diamonds. Declarer now cashes the ace-king of clubs, enters dummy with a trump and leads the jack of clubs. When East follows low, declarer discards his remaining diamond. West can do no better than win and return a club for East to ruff.

Declarer overruffs, enters dummy with a trump and leads the queen of diamonds. If East covers, declarer ruffs, enters dummy with a trump and discards a heart on the jack of diamonds. Now he can lead a heart toward his king, playing for an overtrick. But suppose West had the king of diamonds. When East follows low, declarer discards a heart. West wins the king of diamonds, but he can do declarer no harm. There is a trump in dummy to serve as an entry which will allow declarer to discard a second heart on the jack of diamonds, thus limiting his losers to a trick in each side suit.

BRUCE JOHNSTON

DORIS DAY
President of
ARTISTS MUSIC, INC.

proudly congratulates

BRUCE JOHNSTON

on his
GRAMMY AWARDS
nomination for
"SONG OF THE YEAR"

"I WRITE THE SONGS"

Recorded by:

FRANK SINATRA · JOHNNY MATHIS
CAPTAIN and TENNILLE · RAY CONIFF
DAVID CASSIDY · FERRANTE and TEICHER
LENNY DEE · CHARLIE BYRD · *and*

BARRY MANILOW
("Record of the Year" Nominee for "I WRITE THE SONGS")

TERRY MELCHER
Vice President

(BRUCE JOHNSTON is published
exclusively by ARTISTS MUSIC, INC.)

BRUCE JOHNSTON

PIPELINE
by BOB SPICKARD and BRIAN CARMAN

Recorded on CBS by
Bruce Johnston

BRUCE JOHNSTON'S PLANS

FORMER Beach Boy Bruce Johnston has scrapped plans to join forces with Elton John's new Rocket label and has gone into partnership with West Coast producer Terry Melcher.

Johnston telephoned Disc offices from the West Coast last week to talk of his "big gamble."

The new label, so far without a name, will be totally independent of the major companies, handling its own coast-to-coast distribution.

Johnston and Melcher are currently buying property in Beverly Hills in which they will install 16-track recording facilities.

Among first recordings will be an album by a new three-piece called California, led by Dean Torrence—formerly of Jan and Dean.

Johnston and Melcher also plan solo albums. "We'll also be asking Doris Day (Melcher's mother) if she'd like to record with us. It sounds as though she could do any Bee Gees songs," said Johnston.

The pair plan to invest $1 million during the first year, a further million the following year—if necessary—and if capital is still needed they'll turn to a major label for financing.

"But I know it will work," said Johnston. "We're going to gamble just like A & M did ten years ago."

He said he would suggest to the Beach Boys that they start a similar undertaking when their Warner Bros. contract expires in a year's time.

composer and have yet to find a name.

First dates are early June in Denmark, followed by concerts in Germany and Switzerland.

TERRY MELCHER shares a table with Cass & group with Beatles.

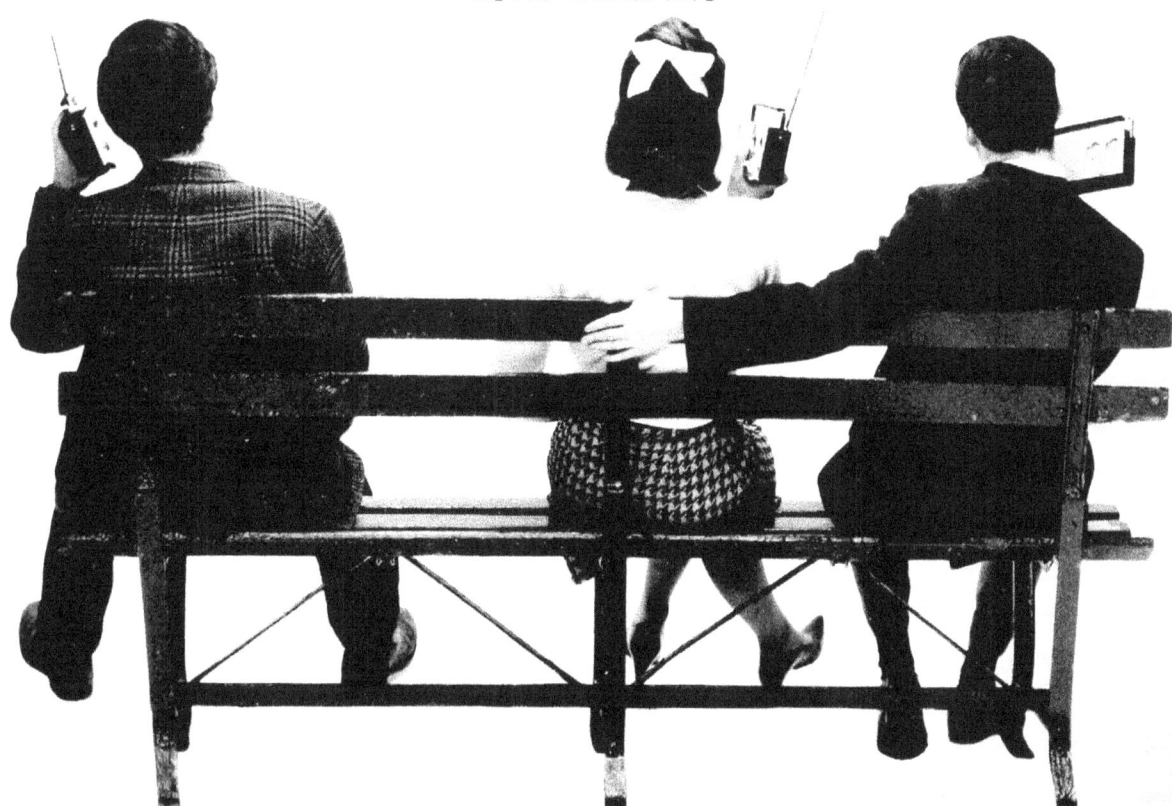

BRUCE & TERRY

your profits...

With these dynamic duos!

BRUCE and TERRY
and their top-40 single sound
"COME LOVE"

CHAD and JEREMY
and their top-40 single sound
"TEENAGE FAILURE"

ON COLUMBIA RECORDS®

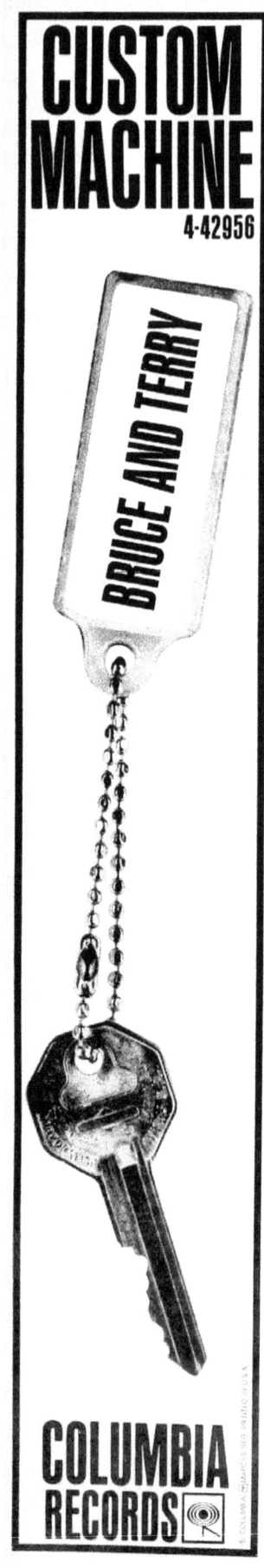

BRUCE AND TERRY
(Columbia 42956)

● "CUSTOM MACHINE" (1:35) [Sea Of Tunes — BMI — Wilson] Bruce and Terry could cash in on the hot rod craze with this sleek Jan & Dean-styled opus. The side sports a racing arrangement with appropriate choral-ork assist. Strong sales and airplay potential.

"THREE WINDOW COUPE" (1:51)
[Screen Gems, Columbia BMI—Berry, Christian
"HOT ROD U.S.A." (2:24) [T.M. BMI—Darin, Melcher]
THE RIP CHORDS (Columbia 43035)

The Rip Chords should quickly zoom back up smash lists with this powerful follow-up to "Hey Little Cobra." This time, they're riding with a "Three Window Coupe" that's loaded with the thumping, coin-catching sounds of "Cobra." and "Drag City," etc. More of the same potent, tailored-for-teens hot rod stuff on the bottom lid. Two-sided sales dynamite here.

"HEY LITTLE COBRA"—Rip Cords—Columbia CL 2151
The Rip Chords tag this power-packed Columbia album after the giant single of "Hey Little Cobra" and include eleven other hard-driving hot rod items. The duo's wide-range, vocal talents carry them in good stead in top-flight, rhythmic renditions of "Here I Stand," "Little Deuce Coupe" and "Drag City." Album has enough built-in success ingredients to score heavily.

BRUCE & TERRY

1,000,000 H.P.*!
*HIT POTENTIAL

CUSTOM MACHINE
BY BRUCE & TERRY
4-42956

COLUMBIA SINGLES SELL

RIP CHORDS

WHEN JOANNA LOVED ME
Tony Bennett
4-42996

TODAY
The New Christy Minstrels
4-43000

LOUIE GO HOME
Paul Revere and The Raiders
4-43008

NOMAD
Louis Armstrong and Dave Brubeck
4-43032

THREE WINDOW COUPE
The Rip Chords
4-43035

WRONG FOR EACH OTHER
Andy Williams
4-43015

COLUMBIA RECORDS

"WHEN JOANNA LOVED ME"
4-42996
TONY BENNETT

"TODAY"
4-43000
THE NEW CHRISTY MINSTRELS

"LOUIE-GO HOME"
4-43008
PAUL REVERE AND THE RAIDERS

"THREE WINDOW COUPE"
4-43035
THE RIP CHORDS

"WRONG FOR EACH OTHER"
4-43015
ANDY WILLIAMS

COLUMBIA RECORDS

COLUMBIA

CUSTOM MACHINE
Bruce and Terry
4-42956

I CAN'T STOP TALKING ABOUT YOU
Steve and Eydie
4-42932

THE GRASSHOPPER
Amadeo and His Indian Harps
4-42918

I'LL SEARCH MY HEART
Johnny Mathis
4-42916

SAGINAW, MICHIGAN
Lefty Frizzell
4-42924

RIP CHORDS

YOUR JANUARY SINGLES SELL CHART

☑ **A Fool Never Learns** / Andy Williams
4-42950

☑ **Hey Little Cobra** / The Rip Chords
4-42921

☑ **I Can't Stop Talking About You** / Steve and Eydie
4-42932

☑ **The Little Boy** / Tony Bennett
4-42931

☑ **Saginaw, Michigan** / Lefty Frizzell
4-42924

☑ **Little Boxes** / Pete Seeger
4-42940

☑ **Hootenanny Saturday Night** / The Brothers Four
4-42927

☑ **That Boy Is Messin' Up My Mind** / The Orchids
4-42913

☑ **The Grasshopper (El Cigarron)** / Amadeo and His Indian Harps
4-42918

☑ **I'll Search My Heart** / Johnny Mathis
4-42916

COLUMBIA SINGLES SELL

GET THE PICTURE... 5 HOT SINGLES!

"WRONG FOR EACH OTHER"
ANDY WILLIAMS
4-43015

"WHEN JOANNA LOVED ME"
TONY BENNETT
4-42996

"TODAY"
THE NEW CHRISTY MINSTRELS
4-43000

"THREE WINDOW COUPE"
THE RIP CHORDS
4-43035

"LOUIE—GO HOME"
PAUL REVERE & THE RAIDERS
4-43008

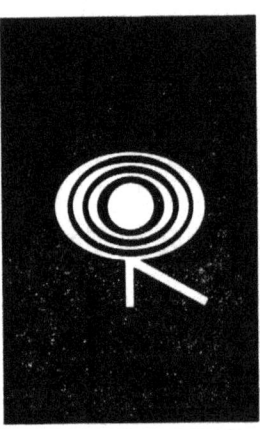

COLUMBIA RECORDS

FROM THE SMASH SINGLE COMES THE NEW HIT ALBUM!

(THE RIP CHORDS NOW ON TOUR WITH THE DICK CLARK SHOW)

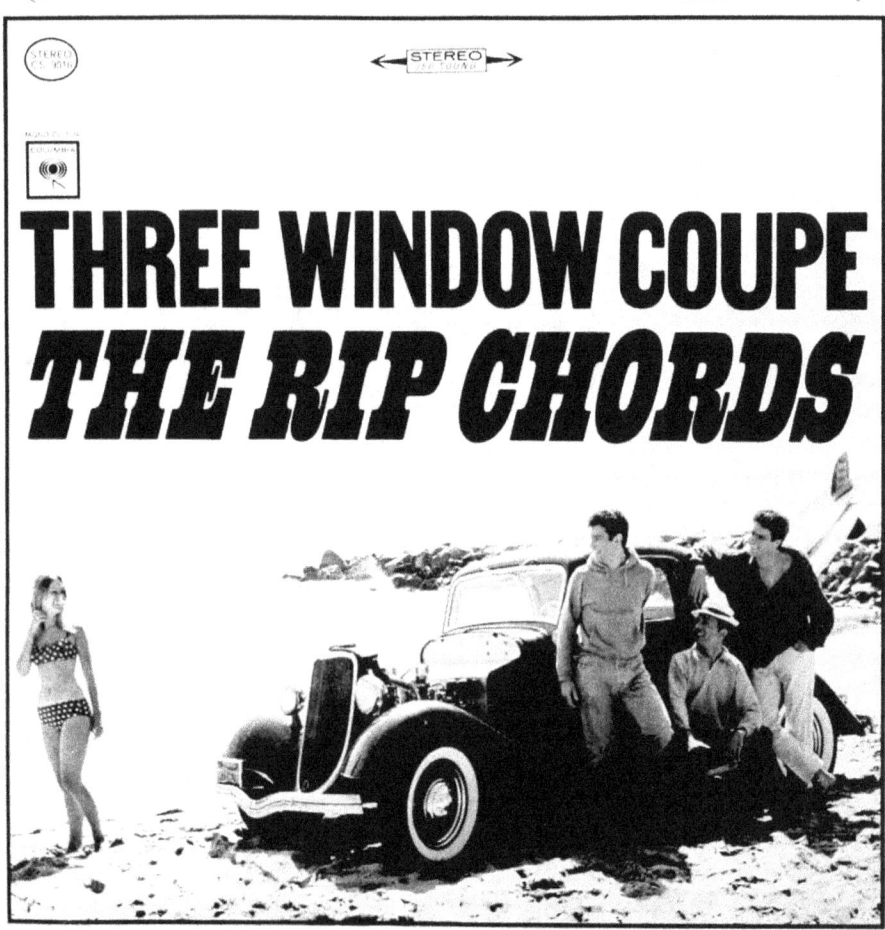

ON COLUMBIA RECORDS

RIP CHORDS

KLOS 1964 CARAVAN OF STARS

Featuring:
- GENE PITNEY
- BRIAN HYLAND
- MAJOR LANCE
- DICKIE CUPS
- BOBBY FREEMAN
- REFLECTIONS
- RIP CHORDS
- JELLY BEANS
- PREMIERS
- PAUL PETERSON
- CRYSTALS

Plus Many Others
Over 50 Name Entertainers

SUNDAY AUGUST 9th 8:00 P.M.

CIVIC AUDITORIUM

Tickets On Sale:
Riedling: Downtown
Record Roundup
Record Rendezvous
(both locations)
Morr's Barber Shop

Success Unlimited Promotion

WAR MEMORIAL
Johnstown, Pa.

Dick Clark — 1964 Caravan Of Stars

July 8th   8:00 P.M.

Mike Clifford	The Coasters	The Crystals
The Dixie Cups	Dean & Jean	Brenda Holloway
Brian Hyland	The Kasuals	Major Lance Gene Pitney
George McCannon	The Reflections	The Rip Chords
Round Robin	The Shirelles	The Supremes

Adm. $1.50 Advance Sale $2.00 At door
Advance ticket sale at: Stapleton's Restaurant

RIP CHORDS

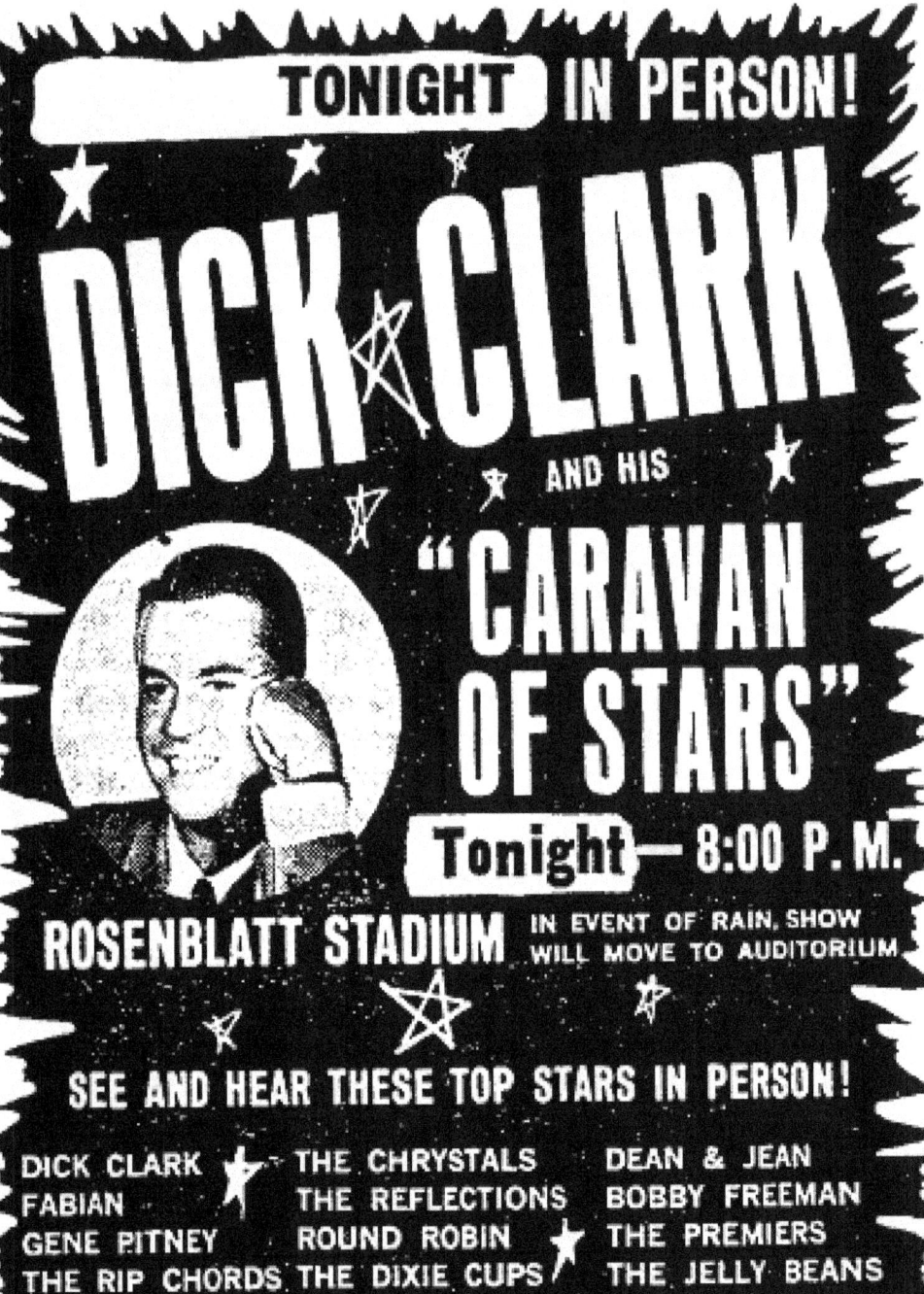

FLAME

Flames stay hot, thanks to a Beach Boy

By JOHN HALSALL

GETTING a gig at London's Revolution club, being seen and raved over by a Beach Boy, transported to America to record with the Beach Boys' company — and being the second band on their forthcoming British tour . . . that's the luck that befell South African group, the Flames.

The easy way to the top? Not really, when it's one of the very few good things that's happened to a determined band that has been dogged by officialdom and bad luck since its inception.

Back in South Africa the Flames' big trouble was always that they were coloured. In South Africa the rules are simple; no black artist may perform before a white audience, and vice versa.

Yet, a few years ago, while these same rules applied, they were treated very lightly — and black groups did in fact play before white audiences. And ironically, it was the Flames who destroyed the "tolerant" scene and made the authorities tighten up.

Here's how it happened.

In 1966 a club I was running at the Al-Fresco Hotel in Durban was going through a thin time, and looked very much like closing down. How could it be saved?

The reply from Durban teenagers who were questioned about the problem was always the same: "Get us the Flames and the place will be packed every night . . ."

A rule checking session was started . . . solicitors engaged and Government departments hammered . . . and they found no rule to stop the Flames playing the club.

Contracts were signed and, on the first night, over 500 people had to be turned away from the door. This situation went on for over a year; at one point they left the Al Fresco for a tour of Capetown and the club was empty for a week.

New recording contracts were negotiated and every Flames record, both singles and albums, soared to the top of the South African chart.

And then the ominous signs began to appear . . . their popularity amongst the whites, projected by the kids through their parents, had set Government wheels in motion. You could almost imagine the top bods saying 'we can't have our kids idolising a kaffir group! Eventually, new legislation was passed forbidding coloured entertainers from appearing before white audiences without specific permission.

Flames made their decision. One last BIG tour of the Republic before the law became final and they split for England.

They couldn't have picked a worse time — right in the middle of the terrible controversy over the Asians from Kenya who were flowing, unstemmed, into Britain at the time. Three of the Flames are Asian and that was good enough for the Immigration people. And anyway, if you're a foreigner with "Musician" stamped on your passport and you happen to have guitars, drums and about two tons of equipment with you, you haven't a chance, whether you're coloured or not!

The Flames were held pending a quick return to South Africa.

On Beach Boys tour—the FLAMES (from left) Blondie Chaplin, Brother Fataar, Steve Fataar, Ricky Fataar.

Appeals were made, but apparently to no effect. Then, just as they were about to leave for the coach that was to take them to London Airport, Brother, the Flames' bass guitarist came in and said, with a half smile on his face, "I don't know what you lot are going to do but I'm going to London," a last minute reprieve had been achieved!

But their troubles still weren't over! For three months they held discussions with the Musicians Union, who, although sympathetic, were wary. Eventually, they got their work-permits.

The net result of their first appearances was instant success. But they didn't do any recording — simply because they were sharp enough to realise that they had to build a reputation among British audiences to get the best deal.

Flames became firm favourites at the Revolution, Blaises and many other London venues. Their music was raw soul, good to dance to and good to listen to.

Jim Carter-Fea, manager of the Revolution and Blaises, personally arranged for Carl Wilson of the Beach Boys to fly from Paris during their 1969 European tour, specifically to hear the Flames. Carl was so impressed that he immediately arranged for them to follow the Beach Boys back to Los Angeles to record under the then embryo Brother label.

This was the offer that the Flames had been waiting for. They've been in the States ever since, concentrating on writing and producing records. Their first single, "See The Light," is, at the time of writing, bubbling under the U.S. hot 100. It should be released here to co-incide with the Beach Boys tour, on which the Flames will be the support group.

When you hear it you'll know their trouble has been worth it!

FLAME

FLAME

The Flame

They are four young men from South Africa and are spreading a unique blend of rock around the globe with their new Brother Records album, The Flame.

In South Africa they made a record and personal appearances and took the country by storm. At once their record was a success and they went on to make other records. One of their recordings held the number one position for fourteen weeks in South Africa.

After this they gathered themselves up and took off for Great Britain and once into clubs in London won a new audience of admirers. Brian Jones (late star of The Rolling Stones); the Bee Gees, and Carl Wilson of The Beach Boys heard them and each offered an opportunity of a record contract, but Flame took Carl Wilson's offer.

It took a long time before the United States immigration officials allowed the Flame into America. But when they arrived, recording began. The results are found in the group's Brother album, which is distributed in America by King; in South Africa by the label the group started on, Trutone; and in the rest of the World by EMI.

The Flame love concerts and clubs — anywhere they can spread the good vibes that come from their original rock songs. In Los Angeles, they've played to cheering audiences at the Whiskey A Go Go and at the Troubador; they've already completed a five-week, ten thousand mile, twenty city promotional tour in the US, and a tour of England, Europe, and South Africa and now a concert tour of the key American cities including tonight's performance here in Los Angeles.

From all indications of past events the era of Flame has begun lighting the light of originality on millions of record turntables.

Blondie Chaplin — lead vocal and guitar
Brother Fataar — bass guitar, vocal
Ricky Fataar — percussion, vocal
Steve Fataar — rhythmn guitar, and lead vocal

RON ALTBACH

PRODUCED BY - Ron Altbach
Engineer - Jeff Peters

SIDE ONE
"DISCO SYMPHONY" - by Mike Love & Ron Altbach
Publishing - Mesa Lane (ASCAP) & Challove (BMI)
Lead Vocal - Suzanne Wallach
Bass - Kevin Brandon
Guitar - Jerry Donahue
Drums - Kim Calkins
Keyboard & Synthesizer - Paul Fauerso

"YOU CAN COUNT ON LOVE" - by Mike Love & Ron Altbach
Publishing - Mesa Lane (ASCAP) & Challove (BMI)
Lead Vocal - Paul Fauerso
Bass - Kevin Brandon
Guitar - Jerry Donahue
Drums - Kim Calkins
Keyboard & Synthesizer - Paul Fauerso

SIDE TWO
"CALIFORNIA GIRLS" - by Brian Wilson & Mike Love
Publishing - Irving Music, Inc. (BMI)
Sax - Charles Lloyd
Guitar - Ed Carter
Bass - Wells Kelly
Drums - Michael Kowalski

"PARTY GIRL" - By Mike Love & Ron Altbach
Publishing - Mesa Lane (ASCAP) & Challove (BMI)
Lead Vocal - Suzanne Wallach
Bass - Kevin Brandon
Guitar - Jerry Donahue
Drums - Kim Calkins
Keyboard & Synthesizer - Paul Fauerso

"FIRST LOVE" - by Paul Fauerso
Publishing - So Far, So Good
Keyboards - Paul Fauerso
Guitar - Tim Weston
Lead Vocal - Paul Fauerso
Bass - Kevin Brandon
Drums - Kim Calkins

Jerry Donahue appears courtesy of Chinnichap
Produced by Ron Altbach for Lovesongs Productions, Inc.
for AMREC Enterprises
©℗1979 AMREC Enterprises

Art Direction/Design
Lauren Garza
Photography
Larry Champman

DINO DESI & BILLY

DINO, DESI & BILLY
GIANT SOUVENIR BOOK
Regular $1.25
ONLY $1.00
(including postage)

Includes all the facts about Dino, Desi & Billy—

- getting the full treatment in Hawaii — leis, lipstick and showers
- what their famous parents think of their success
- the type of girls they like and DISLIKE
- their first TV show and how it happened
- their favorite cars
- their musical backgrounds
- pictures of their family and fans
- and much, much more

Just fill in the coupon below, enclose $1.00 and it's all yours.

```
SOUVENIR BOOK
6290 Sunset Blvd., Suite 504
Hollywood 28, Calif.

Name_____
Address_____
City_____ State_____ Zip____
Enclosed find $1.00 cash ☐ ... check ☐ ... money order ☐
```

On The BEAT

By Louise Criscione

Heard quite an interesting story from Mr. Hinsche (Billy's father) on how Billy finally got his first electric guitar. It seems that Dino Jr. had acquired a brand new Fender guitar and so, naturally, his friend Billy felt that he too should have an electric guitar. Billy hinted to his father, who informed him that *he* was not about to spend $500 on a new guitar, especially since Billy could not even play one!

However, Mr. Hinsche did give his son's request a little more thought and finally came up with a solution to the problem. So, early one morning he and Billy made a trip down to one of the Main Street hock shops and purchased a $65 guitar!

After obtaining his precious guitar, Billy set out to teach himself to play (and play pretty well too). Now that Billy is such a star he has four secretaries answering his fan mail—and he finally did get that $500 guitar!

Puts Down Violence

In his hotel room, Donovan confided to the *BEAT* that: "I don't think violence is a pretty thing or bearable, and our children shouldn't see or learn it."

One English reporter wrote that the Byrds are "the greatest impact-making group to emerge from America for years."

"On The Beat" reported about a month ago that John Lennon had purchased a new Rolls Royce which he had completely blacked-out.

... BILLY HINSCHE

Apparently the London police do not read "On The Beat" for as John was speeding (Well, maybe not *speeding*) through London, he was stopped by the police because they thought that his blacked-out car was "suspicious."

Now how could anyone possibly think that a shaded Lennon in a Blacked-out Rolls was suspicious? I mean, how could *anyone*?

DINO DESI & BILLY

BEAT Photo by C. Boyd

Will Success Spoil Three Little Rich Boys?

By Beverly Akins

Born with the traditional silver spoons in their mouths, Dino, Desi and Billy have no rags to riches story.

Dino is the son of Dean Martin and Desi is the son of Lucille Ball and Desi Arnez. Because the parents of the third member of the trio are not famous Hollywood stars, the question of the hour seems to be: "Who is Billy's father and what does he do?" The answer is simple—Billy's father is a man named Mr. Hinsche and he is an extremely successful Southern California businessman.

And now that we have the parentage thing all cleared up, we can go on to the boys themselves.

Two Secretaries

The three have captured the young record-buying audience in such a tremendous way that each one of the boys has *two* girls answering the huge amount of fan mail which is being written to them daily. Quite an achievement when you consider they've only released one record, "I'm a Fool."

The BEAT caught up with them at a recording session where they were putting the finishing touches on their first album. During the interview, the sheet music arrived causing quite a bit of excitement among the three. They huddled over one song in particular, "Like A Rolling Stone." The song will be featured in their album, and this was the first time that they had actually been able to make out all the lyrics!

School First

The boys, of course, are still attending school and this makes things a little rough. But whether it's rough or not, all of the boys' parents have decided that school definitely comes first. Like it or not, all three went to summer school and in September all three will march on back to school, full time.

Billy, who is 14, will attend Loyola in the fall. Dino, who is 13, will go to Rexford (a private school) and then join Billy at Loyola. Poor Desi is, to his frustration, still only twelve and, therefore, still attending Beverly Hills Catholic School. The other two boys consider this situation hilarious, but Desi himself is not so happy about being the "baby" of the group.

Future Plans

The future seems a long way off for the boys, but they *are* giving it a little bit of thought. In fact, Dino has his mind all made up: "I want to produce records," he states positively. Desi is not quite so sure, but he does know one thing: "I'll go on playing the drums. Oh, and I'd like to live in Hawaii."

Had he ever been to Hawaii before? "Yes, lots of times." To which Billy and Dino teased: "Oh, yeah, Desi's a world traveler"!

As for Billy's future, he says: "It's kind of early. I haven't really decided yet."

In the immediate future, Desi is eagerly awaiting their forthcoming trip to Hawaii, while Billy is looking forward to an up-coming stint in the Jan & Dean movie, "Easy Come, Easy Go."

Would this be the first time the boys had ever faced the Hollywood cameras?

Billy said: "I've done a couple of things. I was in a movie with Barbara Rush when I was five years old." Reminded that he had said a "couple of things" but had only volunteered information about one, Billy admitted that acting had made such an impression on him that he had forgotten what else he had "starred" in!

Acting Experience

Desi said that this would not be his first acting experience either: "I was on the 'Lucy Show' about five times. Then I was on 'Truth or Consequences'. I was behind this curtain playing the drums, and the contestants were supposed to guess how old I was. They were all guessing ages like 54"!

Well, that leaves Dino—had he ever acted before? "I never did anything exciting," he moaned.

Billy had obviously been giving those "couple of things" some more thought for all of a sudden he blurted out: "I just remembered that I was a swimming baby with Esther Williams one time!"

All three of the boys have current pet peeves. Dino dislikes "corny jokes about our hair and our clothes"; Desi dislikes "dumb people"; and Billy dislikes "waiting to go on stage—that gets you."

No Allowances

As all of the boys come from well-to-do families, money is no problem. But do the boys receive an allowance or what? Desi says: "No, I've never had an allowance." Billy added that none of them get an allowance, but "when we need some money, we just ask for it." To which Dino replied: "Yeah, we ask for it, but we don't always get it"!

Dino, Desi and Billy each have their favorites in the entertainment field. Desi names the Byrds, Chad & Jeremy, and "for the movies I like Jack Lemmon and, of course, my mother"!

All the while Desi was answering the question, Dino was standing beside me repeating "Byrds" over and over in my ear until I somehow got the idea that he liked the Byrds a whole lot!

Billy lists his favorite entertainer as Bob Dylan, pronouncing him "really cool."

Group favorites are the Beatles and the Beach Boys. "And don't forget the Byrds", Dino quickly added. And Billy piped up with "and Bob Dylan." And Desi? He just laughed.

Free Time

The boys do not have much free time, but when that rarity does occur, they all enjoy doing something different. Desi can probably be found either surfing or go-carting. You might find Billy with his ever-present guitar strapped securely around his neck and coming up with new sounds on it.

And Dino will be found riding motorcycles. The BEAT reporter brought up the fact that he couldn't ride motorcycles because he was not yet sixteen. "Well, up in Palm Springs you can ride around the hills, and we own a lot of property up there," Dino explained. That last statement drew scornful looks and ridiculing sighs from the other two.

If you get the impression that a lot of teasing goes on among Dino, Desi and Billy—you're right. The boys have come a long way in a short time. They're young and they're impressionable—it would not be hard for them to become swell-headed and completely taken with themselves.

Kept In Line

But because there are three of them, and because they do not hestitate to put each other down for making what they consider to be a conceited or phony remark—I don't think that they will ever fall into that balloon-headed and egotistical trap. They bring each other down too much for that.

If they continue to progress as they have been doing, Dino, Desi and Billy are just liable to out-shoot everyone else in the record business. They have certainly made a good start as it is. They have appeared with the Beach Boys, they have completed a "Dean Martin Show" which will be aired on October 14, and they are set for a "Sammy Davis Jr. Special" which will be shown on Thanksgiving Day.

Already, people are starting to point a finger at Dean Martin and say: "I know you—you're Dino's father." Sounds a lot like an indication of big things to come for Dino, Desi and Billy—doesn't it?

MURRAY WILSON

DINO, DESI & BILLY say they're not "The Lovin' Kind" but **The BEAT** found them to be pretty lovable characters! They sure look lovable here. Okay, and now back to the schoolbooks, boys.

FAMED SONS, Dino Martin (left) and Desi Arnez (right) along with Billy, the son of a California contractor, combined talents and came out with a hit, "I'm a Fool." The three should have no trouble making their own names in the pop music world.

On The BEAT

By Louise Criscione

Heard quite an interesting story from Mr. Hinsche (Billy's father) on how Billy finally got his first electric guitar. It seems that Dino Jr. had acquired a brand new Fender guitar and so, naturally, his friend Billy felt that he too should have an electric guitar. Billy hinted to his father, who informed him that *he* was not about to spend $500 on a new guitar, especially since Billy could not even play one!

However, Mr. Hinsche did give his son's request a little more thought and finally came up with a solution to the problem. So, early one morning he and Billy made a trip down to one of the Main Street hock shops and purchased a $65 guitar!

After obtaining his precious guitar, Billy set out to teach himself to play (and play pretty well too). Now that Billy is such a star he has four secretaries answering his fan mail—and he finally did get that $500 guitar!

Puts Down Violence

In his hotel room, Donovan confided to the *BEAT* that: "I don't think violence is a pretty thing or bearable, and our children shouldn't see or learn it."

One English reporter wrote that the Byrds are "the greatest impact-making group to emerge from America for years."

"On The Beat" reported about a month ago that John Lennon had purchased a new Rolls Royce which he had completely blacked-out.

Apparently the London police do not read "On The Beat" for as John was speeding (Well, maybe not *speeding*) through London, he was stopped by the police because they thought that his blacked-out car was "suspicious."

Now how could anyone possibly think that a shaded Lennon in a Blacked-out Rolls was suspicious? I mean, how could *anyone*?

. . . **BILLY HINSCHE**

Junior Success—Dino, Desi And Billy Style

Dino, Desi, and Billy . . . a modern success story, junior style. Although the boys are just fourteen years old, they have already managed to come up with two hit records — with their first two releases.

The boys are currently concentrating on their educations, which is of the utmost importance to all three. For this reason, it is very difficult for them to make many personal appearances or to make any plans for extended personal appearance tours around the country. Their personal manager, Mac Gray, explains that "school keeps them all very busy, and everything else is secondary to them right now."

It may be secondary, but that doesn't prevent them from receiving several large mailbags of fan letters daily from their many fans —both young and not-so-young— for which they must have two girls who do nothing but handle their mail.

In just a short time, the boys will again go into a recording studio to produce their next single, and working as producer on the session will be a man named Lee Hazelwood, who was also responsible for Nancy Sinatra's record, "These Boots Are Made For Walkin'." Also, there is a very strong possibility that the boys may make a motion picture—the first for all three—for Paramount in the near future.

. . . **DINO, DESI AND BILLY**

AT HOME WITH BILLY HINSCHE

ALL PHOTOS BY GLORIA STAVERS.

The handsome house in which Billy lives is in Beverly Hills, California. And there's Billy on the steps.

"It sure took you a long time to get here! C'mon in and let me show you around."

"First, let's have a snack."

"Care to hear a tune or two before we make the tour?"

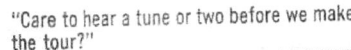

"Personally, I like my music on an instrument I can strum."

BILLY HINSCHE

"My trophy chest. The awards are for Little League Baseball."

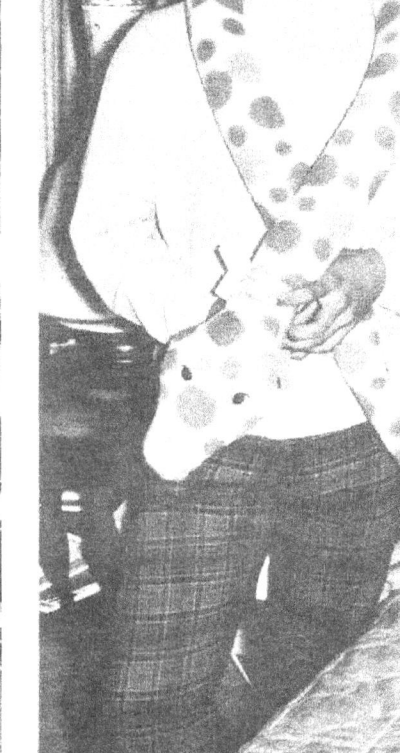

"A fan sent me this wrap-around snake."

"Homework. Ugh."

"Once in a while I build up the energy to clean my mosaic tile swimming pool."

DINO DESI & BILLY

Contract Blank

AMERICAN FEDERATION OF MUSICIANS
OF THE UNITED STATES AND CANADA
MUSICIANS UNION LOCAL 47, LOS ANGELES, CALIFORNIA
817 VINE STREET, LOS ANGELES, CALIFORNIA, 90038

THIS CONTRACT for the personal services of musicians, made this **9th** day of **February**, 19**68**, between the undersigned purchaser* of music (hereinafter called the "Employer") and **three (3)** musicians (hereinafter called "employees").*
(Including the Leader)

The employer engages the employees as musicians severally on the terms and conditions below, and as further specified on reverse side. The leader represents that the musicians already designated have agreed to be bound by said terms and conditions. The employer agrees that musicians may be selected by the leader. Each employee yet to be chosen shall be so bound by said terms and conditions upon agreeing to accept his employment. Each musician may enforce this agreement.

The employees severally agree to render collectively to the employer services as musicians in the orchestra under the leadership of (Please Print) _____ as follows:

Print Name of Place of Engagement **Atlantic City Steel Pier**
Print Address of Place of Engagement **Steel Pier, Atlantic City**
Print Date(s) and Hours of Employment **July 20th and July 21st, one 45 minute show each night, three shows per day**

Print Type of Engagement (specify whether dance, concert, revue, theatrical, sports event, etc.) **Concert**
WAGES AGREED UPON INCLUDING TOTAL PENSION CONTRIBUTION, $**7,000.00**

This wage includes expenses agreed to be reimbursed by the employer in accordance with the attached schedule, or a schedule to be furnished the employer on or before the date of engagement.
To be paid **To be paid in full after the last performance**
(Specify when payments are to be made)

Upon request by the American Federation of Musicians of the United States and Canada (herein called the "Federation") or the Local Union in whose jurisdiction the employees shall perform hereunder, the employer either shall make advance payment hereunder or shall post an appropriate bond.

Print Employee's Name (As on Social Security card) Last, First, Initial	Local Union No.	Social Security No.	Wages	A.F.M. & E.P.W. Fund Contribution
1. Martin, Dino	47			
2. (Leader)				
3. Arnaz, Desi	47			
4. Hinsche, Billy	47			
5.				
6.				
7.				
8.				
9.				
10.				

ABEL HOLDING CO., INC. T/A
Atlantic City Steel Pier
Print Employer's Name (Title)
X _____ 2/13/68
Authorized Signature Date
George Hamid, Jr., Vice Pres.

Boardwalk and Steel Pier
Print Street Address
Atlantic City, N.J.   609-587-1496
City   State   Phone

DINO, DESI & BILLY   47
Print Leader's Name   Local No.
X _____
Leader's Signature   Date
327 North Rodeo Drive
Print Street Address
Beverly Hills, Calif.   271-8193
City   State   Phone
X _____
Signature of approved A.F. of M. BOOKING AGENT   Phone

*This contract does not conclusively determine the person liable to report and pay employment taxes and similar employer levies under rulings of the U. S. Internal Revenue Service and of some state agencies.

Note—Additional Terms on Reverse Side
(OVER)

FORM B-2B Cal. (47) Rev. 1-68

BRIAN WILSON

BRIAN WILSON

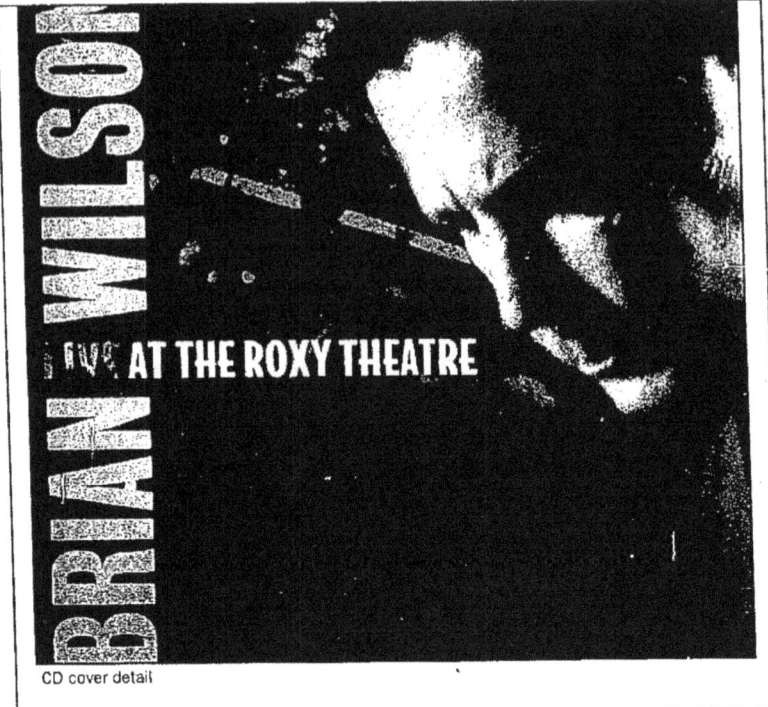

CD cover detail

Brian Wilson's double disc **Live at the Roxy Theater** is an extremely enjoyable listen even though relatively little new is going on.

For the most part Wilson and his band play his oldies including several songs he rerecorded for his *I Just Wasn't Made for These Times* studio album a few years ago. The latter redos include *'Til I Die, In My Room, Love and Mercy* and *Caroline No.*

While the tone of that album is melancholy, Roxy is more balanced, with Wilson throwing in such good-time Beach Boys tunes as *All Summer Long, California Girls* and the still majestic *I Get Around.*

Wilson also pulls out some BB obscurities — *The Little Girl I Once Knew, Please Let Me Wonder* and *Kiss Me Baby* — which show his brooding musical-experimentation mojo was working even before *Pet Sounds.*

That critically acclaimed 1966 Beach Boys album is well-represented, including versions of the album's two instrumentals, the title song and *Let's Go Away for Awhile.*

Wilson covers a song by his hero Phil Specter (*Be My Baby*); and a Barenaked Ladies' ditty called — yes — *Brian Wilson,* which pokes fun at Wilson's well-known eccentricities: living-room sandbox, years spent in bed.

The new live discs contain a smattering of recent tunes. *This Isn't Love,* co-written with *Pet Sounds* lyricist **Tony Asher**, is a sweet tune — and sounds better if you forget its first appearance: in a Flintstones movie. And *Lay Down Burden* — which first appeared on Brian's previous solo album, *Imagination* — is a mournful tribute to Wilson's late brother Carl.

Wilson's new band is virtually flawless, both instrumentally and vocally, without sounding sterile. But most importantly, Wilson, who stopped touring with the band early on, actually sounds like he's having fun onstage.

Live at the Roxy Theater is available only from www.brianwilson.com.

Meanwhile Rhino Records just rereleased Wilson's wonderful 1988 self-titled solo record complete with studio outtakes and unheard songs.

And to top it off, this summer Capitol Records rereleased and repackaged The Beach Boys' entire 1970s and '80s output, fitting 11 albums onto five single CDs on one double-disc package. The rereleases include:

▼ **Brian Wilson.** Some fans refer to this one as the "Dr. Landy" album because Wilson's then-live-in shrink-guru-weight watcher, **Eugene Landy**, is listed as executive producer and Brian clearly was under his sway. Wilson's family called Landy a thief and a Svengali and indeed California authorities eventually yanked Landy's license and prohibited him from contact with Wilson.

That said, the record is one of Wilson's finest. *Love and Mercy* is the standout song, hands down. But *Brian Wilson* contains lots of gorgeous tunes — the mystical *There's So Many;* the wistful *Melt Away;* the wacky Pee-Wee Herman-does-a-Western *Rio Grande.*

The bonus tracks — such as *Too Much Sugar,* a Wilson sermon on physical fitness — are interesting but not of the same caliber as the songs that made the original cut. True fans should appreciate the included demos and rough mixes as behind-the-curtain peeks at the wizard at work.

▼ **Sunflower/Surf's Up.** Some real gems are here, including two songs that sprang from the legendary musical abortion *Smile* (*Cool Water* from *Sunflower;* and the *Surf's Up* title cut, which probably is my favorite Wilson song).

There's *Add Some Music to Your Day* (another highlight on the new live album); *At My Window;* and two Carl Wilson classics from *Surf's Up: Feel Flows* and *Long Promised Road.* Despite some ill-advised attempts at protest songs, *Surf's Up* is the strongest of the BB reissues.

▼ **Carl & The Passions: So Tough/Holland.** This is the second time *So Tough* has been packaged with a far superior album. In 1972 *So Tough* came out with a reissued *Pet Sounds.* And now *So Tough* is in a two-disc set with *Holland.*

Steve Terrell
Music Critic

Maybe that's why I don't find much memorable here — except the upbeat *Marcella;* and *Hold On Dear Brother,* an embarrassing stab at imitating The Band.

Holland, simply put, is one of The BBs' finest. Not since their early days do the Boys sound more like a true band. The standout songs are *Sail On Sailor* and *The Trader.*

▼ **The Beach Boys in Concert.** Brian is present only in spirit on this underrated concert record. But the other BBs do themselves proud. They prove they can play *Pet Sounds* songs live after all. **Al Jardine** does a fine job with *She Still Believes in Me* and Carl fills in perfectly for Brian on *Caroline No.*

Heroes and Villains is downright fun and the *Holland* tunes fit in perfectly with the Beach Boys repertoire.

▼ **15 Big Ones/Love You** and **MIU/LA (Light Album).** These later-'70s albums — with the exception of *Love You* — document a band in a serious tailspin. *Love You* has a good balance of summer fun, Brian's introspective sadness, and sheer silliness (*Johnny Carson*). Though the other albums contain some listenable tunes, the less said about them, the better. The overall lack of inspiration is painful.

▼ **Keepin' the Summer Alive/The Beach Boys.** By the time they reach the '80s, The Beach Boys sound like a band of ghosts. ◄

> Some fans refer to 'Brian Wilson' as the 'Dr. Landy' album because Wilson's then-live-in shrink-guru-weight watcher, Eugene Landy, is listed as executive producer and Brian clearly was under his sway

BRian

Associated Press / DOMINIC CONDE

The singing Wilsons *at the S.O.B. club in New York: Dad Brian, the Beach Boy, and daughters Wendy (left) and Carnie sang Wednesday for the Children's Health Fund.*

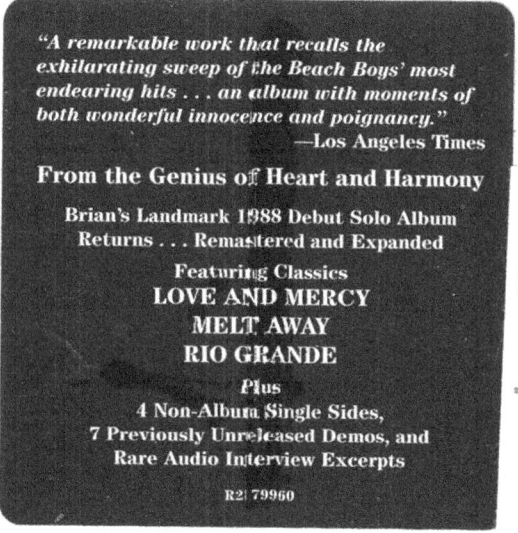

BRIAN WILSON MUSIC CARES INVITATION

BRIAN WILSON MUSIC CARES INVITATION

MusiCares
PERSON
OF THE YEAR

Friday, February 11, 2005
Hollywood Palladium
6215 Sunset Boulevard
Hollywood, California 90028

6:00 PM Silent Auction & Reception
7:30 PM Dinner
9:00 PM Tribute & Concert
         Special Performances by Brian Wilson and Friends

Black Tie Preferred

For table and ticket reservations and/or to place a message in the Tribute Journal, please contact Dana Tomarken at 310.392.3777.

 47th Annual GRAMMY® Week Celebration

MusiCares is a charity founded by The Recording Academy.® Funds raised from the Person of the Year tribute benefit MusiCares' Human Service Programs and draws attention to the important work of the organization.

Brian Wilson is one of popular music's most deeply revered figures and the main creative force behind some of the most cherished music in rock history.

His remarkable musical journey began in the early 1960s when the Southern California native was barely out of his teens. He created some of the most beloved records ever, including nine consecutive gold albums featuring such classics as "Surfer Girl," "I Get Around," "Don't Worry Baby," "Fun, Fun, Fun" and "California Girls" — to name just a few of his more than two dozen Top 40 hits.

In 1966, he produced three records that forever changed the course of popular music. The first was *Pet Sounds*, which is considered by many to be one of the greatest albums ever made. The second was the landmark "Good Vibrations," which Brian famously dubbed a "pocket symphony," and is deemed one of the most important singles of all time. The third was *Smile*, a suite of songs that combined classical composition, multipart harmonies, rock rhythms and an avant-garde sensibility.

Brian had almost completed *Smile* when a combination of circumstances forced him to shelve the project. However, through the decades, even as he battled personal demons and rode the roller coaster of professional ups and downs, he continued to produce musical gems and make beautiful music with the Beach Boys, as a solo artist and with other artists.

As the 20th century came to a close, Brian became a concert performer, conquering his legendary stage fright. His acclaimed *Pet Sounds* tour took this classic album from the studio to concert stages around the world. But Brian never lost sight of the music that had become "the holy grail" of pop — *Smile*. He began to add some of the songs from the album to his live sets and in 2003 announced that he and his chief *Smile* collaborator, Van Dyke Parks, would reunite to complete the album. Conceived as a revolutionary studio record, *Smile* came to life on-stage in a series of concerts throughout the world. As a result, Brian decided to record an all-new studio version of the album and released it in September 2004 to rave reviews.

Over the years, Brian has generously given of his time and talent to causes close to his heart. His philanthropic activities include support of the Carl Wilson Foundation for Cancer Research, and performances at the Adopt-A-Minefield Benefit and Neil Young's Bridge School Concert benefiting those with severe speech and physical impairments.

He has been called the Mozart of Rock, the Gershwin of his generation. But no comparison is necessary; he's Brian Wilson, an American composer, arranger and producer whose work has proved to be as powerful as faith, as timeless as love and as heartfelt as mercy. He has become an honored icon for the musical revolution he created and his inspirational story of strength and perseverance.

MusiCares®
PERSON OF THE YEAR

BRIAN WILSON

BRIAN WILSON MUSIC CARES INVITATION

CITY OF LOS ANGELES
Los Angeles Police Commission Charitable Services Section
(213) 978-1144

- NOT AN ENDORSEMENT BUT FOR INFORMATION ONLY -

INFORMATION CARD NO. B3247

Issued Pursuant to Los Angeles Municipal Code, Chapter 4, Article 4, Philanthropy

MUSICARES FOUNDATION, INC.
3402 Pico Blvd., Santa Monica, CA 90405
Person in charge of appeal: **Kristen Madsen**
For information about this appeal, call: **(310) 392-3777**

Activity: Fundraiser Dinner and Silent Auction on February 11, 2005.

Solicitation Dates: December 10, 2004 to Feb. 11, 2005   Anticipated Expenses: $1,514,722

Purpose: Proceeds will be used to support our financial assistance program to individuals in the Music Community.

Previous Activity: 2004 activity collected a total of $3,174,599 of which $1,850,057 went to charity and $1,324,542 (41.7%) were expenses.

121004

DOOR-TO-DOOR SOLICITATION RESTRICTED TO THE HOURS OF 8 A.M. – 8 P.M.

BRIAN WILSON MUSIC CARES INVITATION

MusiCares PERSON OF THE YEAR
BRIAN WILSON

47TH ANNUAL GRAMMY® WEEK CELEBRATION
Friday, February 11, 2005 • Hollywood Palladium
6:00pm Silent Auction • 7:30pm Dinner • 9:00pm Tribute & Concert

Company Name _____

Contact Name _____

Address _____

City _____

State _____ Zip _____

Phone _____ Fax _____

E-mail _____

TABLE AND TICKET RESERVATIONS

❏ **DIAMOND SPONSOR:** $75,000
 • Three Diamond Tables (36 seats)
 • 4-Color Page in Souvenir Journal

❏ **PLATINUM SPONSOR:** $25,000
 • One Platinum Table (10 seats)
 • 4-Color Page in Souvenir Journal

❏ **SILVER SPONSOR:** $10,000
 • One Silver Table (10 seats)
 • B&W Page in Souvenir Journal

❏ **PLATINUM PLUS SPONSOR:** $50,000
 • Two Platinum Plus Tables (24 seats)
 • 4-Color Page in Souvenir Journal

❏ **GOLD SPONSOR:** $15,000
 • One Gold Table (10 seats)
 • 4-Color Page in Souvenir Journal

❏ **INDIVIDUAL DINNER TICKETS**
 __ Diamond tickets: $7,500 each
 __ Platinum Plus tickets: $5,000 each
 __ Platinum tickets: $2,500 each
 __ Gold tickets: $1,500 each

SOUVENIR JOURNAL ACKNOWLEDGEMENTS OR ADVERTISEMENTS* — AD DEADLINE: JANUARY 14, 2005

❏ INSIDE COVER SPREAD(S): $ 15,000
❏ BACK COVER: $ 10,000
❏ INSIDE COVER(S): $ 8,500
❏ DIVIDER SECTION PAGE(S): $ 7,500
❏ DIAMOND PAGE: $ 5,000
❏ PLATINUM PLUS PAGE: $ 4,500
❏ PLATINUM PAGE: $ 3,500
❏ GOLD PAGE: $ 3,000
❏ SILVER PAGE: $ 2,500

SPECS: Page size is 7 1/2" x 10". 150 line screen. No bleeds. Please provide artwork on disk or e-mail to doritk@grammy.com in the following format: Hi-Res PDF file (preferred format), Quark, Illustrator, or Photoshop, 4-Color or B&W is acceptable.

Acknowledgements are limited to company name, logo, slogan and message to the honoree. Price of an acknowledgement is tax-deductible as a charitable contribution. *Advertisements* include information other than company name, logo, slogan and message to the honoree and are not tax deductible as a charitable contribution. Fair Market Value is the Page Price. A tax letter will be sent following the event listing the fair market value and the tax deductible portion of your contribution. Federal Tax Identification Number: 95-4470909

PAYMENT ARRANGEMENT — Kindly make check payable to the MusiCares Foundation. Payment must be received by January 28, 2005.

❏ Sorry, I am unable to attend. Please accept my donation to the MusiCares Foundation in the amount of $ _____
❏ Check $ _____
❏ Charge amount $ _____ ❏ American Express ❏ MasterCard ❏ Discover ❏ Visa

Card Number _____ Expiration Date _____ Billing Zip Code _____

Name (PLEASE PRINT) _____ Signature _____

For further information, contact: **Dana Tomarken/Dorit Kalev** Tel: 310.392.3777 Fax: 310.392.9699

TICKETS ARE NOT TRANSFERABLE: Person of the Year tickets are for use by the account holder and their invited guest(s) only, are not transferable, and may not be sold or used for promotional, commercial, advertising, or other trade purposes without the express written consent of the MusiCares Foundation. Tickets transferred or re-sold without permission will be revoked and their bearers deemed trespassers. The MusiCares Foundation reserves all legal rights and remedies.

BRIAN WILSON

BIOGRAPHY

It's said that all good things come to those who wait, and Brian Wilson, the first ever solo album from the legendary creator of the "California Sound," is an overdue arrival that fulfills our hopes and expectations---a record that may be as important to the future of popular music as Brian's Beach Boys' work has been in the past.

For those of you who don't devour label credits, a little rock history lesson might be in order. Our first teacher is the original "surfer boy," Brian's late brother Dennis, the Beach Boys' drummer, who said it best: "Brian is the Beach Boys. We're his messengers."

Brian Wilson was the creative force behind the Beach Boys, the most succesful, innovative and influential American band in rock & roll, a group whose timeless music has provided an everlasting soundtrack for a vast and enduring fantasy: a mythical California that Brian conjured forth with his "Good Vibrations."

For Brian, it all began in the modest Wilson family home in Hawthorne, California, a Los Angeles suburb. In the bedroom he shared with his

Sire Records · 75 Rockefeller Plaza · 20th Floor · New York, New York · 10019 · (212) 484-6870
Reprise Records, Inc. · 3300 Warner Boulevard · Burbank, California · 91510 · (818) 953-3223

brothers, Brian taught them to sing the harmonies that he had absorbed from countless listenings to records by the Four Freshmen and Hi-Lo's and from home recording sessions with their mother.

A voracious consumer of music in his youth, Brian was 19 years old when his family band had their first hit in 1961. The Beach Boys recorded their first album in 1962, and by 1963, with Brian running the show, the group became rock's first completely self-contained band.

When the Beach Boys signed with Capitol in 1962, standard industry custom was to assign an A&R man to a group; his job was to select the songs and produce the group's records in the company's own studios. In the early 1960's; record companies hadn't even begun to acknowledge the power of the artist' Brian Wilson, going against every precedent, was the first rock star to tell the record company he was going to do it his way, not their's.

With the backing of his father (the group's manager), Brian became the first and, for a long time, the only rock artist to completely control the musical output of his career. Brian's declaration of independence meant that Brian would pick the songs the Beach Boys would record and choose the musicians who would play on the sessions---he even decided which studio he would use. In 1988, those "rights" are taken for granted; back in 1963, Brian Wilson fought and won the pioneering battle for artistic control in the record business.

But Brian never abused the privilege. Having secured his freedom, Brian kept up his end of the bargain, and the group cranked out an unbelievable quantity of quality music. In those days, groups didn't take four years

BRIAN WILSON

between albums; it took maybe four months. But from their first chart success on Capitol, the pressure was on, and Brian responded with a rapid-fire and virtually uninterrupted string of innovative hits.

From 1962-1966, the Beach Boys scored nearly two dozen Top 40 singles (including three #1 hits) and recorded an incredible twelve albums (ten of which were Top 10, nine gold), virtually all of which were written, arranged and produced by Brian Wilson. In the 1960s, only the unbeatable Beatles had more Top 40 hits than the Beach Boys.

The Beach Boys' sound that Brian created was a deceptively simple, although brand new, combination of basic rock & roll (Chuck Berry guitar) and jazzy, incredibly complex "Four Freshmenesque" vocals. Their style was often imitated, but soaring atop the group's harmonies was the never-duplicated, special ingredient---Brian's trademark falsetto, an otherworldly, heartfelt cry. Brian "washed" the group's vocal blend against Phil Spector's "Wall of Sound," a studio technique that Brian first worshipped, then emulated and eventually refined for his landmark album, Pet Sounds.

But Brian's records, as technically advanced as they were, weren't designed to show off his mastery of the recording studio. What makes his songs still magical today is the pure feeling that Brian instinctively injected into all of the group's records. Whether they expressed a spiritual teen innocence ("Surfer Girl," "Don't Worry Baby"), evoked a fantasy state of mind ("California Girls," "Fun, Fun, Fun") or reflected youth culture ("Surfin' U.S.A.," "I Get Around"), the Beach Boys went to the top of the charts, even in the midst of the Beatlemaniacal '60s.

BRIAN WILSON

Looking back from the context of today's norm---years between releases---it's hard to grasp the supersonic speed of Brian's musical maturation. The evolution of his writing, from the simple elegance of

"Surfer Girl" to the psychedelic signpost of "Good Vibrations," took less than five years; and there were plenty of big musical leaps along the way, like the unusual melancholy beauty of "The Warmth of the Sun," the symphonic opening of "California Girls," and the spirituality of "God Only Knows." In retrospect, it was an amazingly fast, consistent and artistically satisfying progression. Operating in warp drive, Brian's Beach Boys graduated from the garage rock of Surfin' Safari to the fully-realized classical masterpiece of Pet Sounds in less than four years. Remarkably, Pet Sounds, Brian's artistic statement of love, was the group's 12th album in that brief time span.

The first wave of Wilson wizardry peaked in the fall of 1966 when Brian followed Pet Sounds with what he called "a pocket symphony." Even though it was over 3 1/2 minutes long, a practically unheard of length for a single in '66, "Good Vibrations" became an international award-winning, worldwide #1 record.

Cracking the pop hit "time barrier" was radical enough, but what really created a stir in the music community was the way Brian had written and produced "Good Vibrations." Inventing studio techniques as he went along, Brian stitched together "Good Vibrations" in sections taken from different recording sessions, using instruments--including the theremin and cello--and sound combinations that were completely new to rock music.

BRIAN WILSON

The one-two punch of <u>Pet Sounds</u> and "Good Vibrations" put Brian in front of the pack; his artistic and commercial success gave rise to the belief that Brian was rock's one, legitimate genius. The whole world couldn't wait to hear what was coming next; back then, everybody making records wanted to know how Brian was getting such incredible depth and feeling into those recordings. From all over, musicmakers as diverse as Leonard Bernstein and the Beatles came to watch Brian in the studio, hoping to learn the secrets of his powerful magic.

> "<u>Pet Sounds</u> was my inspiration for making <u>Sgt. Pepper's</u>...the big influence... the musical invention... was the big thing for me. I just thought, 'Dear me, this is the album of all time. What are we gonna do'?"
>
> --- Paul McCartney

The Beatles were bowled over by Brian's music, and just as Brian's ambitious experimentation was prodding the Beatles and others to explore new horizons, Brian challenged himself. "Good Vibrations" to Brian wasn't just a peak, it was a plateau, and there seemed to be no limits to the revolutionary musical dreams that he wanted to make a reality. Brian was determined to make a record that would blow everybody's mind, including the Beatles. Unfortunately, Brian's new music ended up blowing his own mind.

But before he did...before it all came to a screeching halt...when "Good Vibrations" was "in the can" but hadn't yet been released, Brian embarked on a musical odyssey of Homeric proportion. Using the form he had created to record "Good Vibrations" and working with a brilliant young lyricist/musician named Van Dyke Parks, Brian went to work on what he said would be "a teenage symphony to God." Originally, it was called <u>Dumb Angel</u>, and the idea was to juxtapose the silly with the spiritual. Then, Brian decided that his next "Good Vibration" would be called Smile. Using his advanced composing style and his unequalled knowledge of the recording studio, Brian set out to make a thematic tribute to the healing powers of his laughter, rock's first full-blown concept album; it was to be Brian's breakthrough.

Never completed, never released, Smile has become the most enigmatic record in the history of rock. Those who heard the "work in progress" swear to this day that Smile would have turned the music world on its ear had it been finished and released on schedule in early 1967.

But Brian, under enormous pressure from inside and all sides, decided that, under the circumstances he couldn't, and wouldn't and didn't have the strength to complete Smile. And so, in mid-1967, he shelved the tapes, relegating his embryonic musical revolution to the land of "might have beens." His eccentric behavior had begun to overshadow his creative abilities, and Brian withdrew from full-time action.

Though Brian's best-known and most influential music comes from his prolific years of 1963-1966, even in semi-retirement, Brian recorded numerous beautiful works including '67's complex "Heroes and Villains", the jazzy Friends LP in 1968, "This Whole World," "Add Some Music" et. al on the harmonically brilliant Sunflower in 1970, the heartbreaking despair of "'Til I Die" on 1971's Surf's Up and the quirky, semi-autobiographicl fairy tale, "Mt. Vernon and Fairway," a 1973 musical "explanation" of his creative difficulties. Each one of those records had wonderful moments, achingly beautiful glimpses of "the gift." With each Beach Boys release, Brian's fans searched the grooved for proof that his incredible talent was intact.

BRIAN WILSON

Ironically, it was Brian's intermittent creativity and puzzling behavior that turned his life into a fascinating mystery. The released music and the myth of Smile combined to create a loyal cult of obsessed followers who were imbued with the passionate belief that one day, Brian would "do it again." But if Brian really was the Mozart of rock, why had his piano fallen silent. Would Brian, everybody wondered, ever again exercise his incredible powers, moreover...could he?

For the most part, Brian has spent the past two decades ducking the issue by staying away from the uncomfortable glare of the public spotlight and by staying outside his natural home, the recording studio. And while he has occasionally written a great song ("Sail On Sailor," "Good Timin'"), in the past dozen years, Brian's best new music has remained locked inside his head and heart. In the world of popular culture, the question is always "What have you done lately?" From Brian Wilson, there has been no satisfactory answer.

Despite the always present questions about his future, Brian's past has influenced just about everybody from the Beatles, the Who, CSN and Neil Young in the '60s to Elton John, the Eagles, ELO and Fleetwood Mac in the '70s to Terence Trent D'Arby, R.E.M. and the Smithereens in the '80s. Brian's classic music has remained potent and important.

Now, over twenty years after creating Pet Sounds, the album that has won the hearts of three generations of musicians, Brian Wilson has come out of his self-imposed, semi-retirement to make his first solo album, Brian Wilson, the brand-new message fresh from the unique musical outpost that is Brian's own special preserve.

BRIAN WILSON

Within eight bars of the first cut on side one, all the concerns and questions evaporate. Clearly, Brian Wilson is a major artistic statement from an inspired musician, a record filled with Brian's love, communicated through the recognizable Wilson magic finally being practiced in the contemporary pop world. Listen...

In essence, Brian Wilson is a two-part album. The first is conventional yet exceptional: ten new songs from Brian that offer wide-ranging observations on the world from his honest, sensitive and often delightfully-amusing perspective. The kaleidoscope of emotions is mind-boggling and occasionally overpowering, from the diary-style toast and prayer of "Love and Mercy" to the celestial dream of "There's So Many," from the Four Freshmen-like "One For The Boys" to the personal revelation of "Melt Away." There's a dance track ("Nighttime"), a retro-rockin' ditty ("Little Children"), technopop humoresque ("Walkin' The Line"), a pep talk ("Baby Let Your Hair Grow Long") and the bright and booming "Let it Shine," which combines the best sounds of two great groups -- ELO and the Beach Boys -- through the creativity of their leaders, Jeff Lynne and Brian Wilson. The last of the first ten is "Meet Me in My Dreams Tonight," an upbeat treat that will bring a smile to your face.

That would be feast enough for Brian Wilson fans. But this album is more than just a collection of songs. What lifts this record from "solid reentry album" to very possibly the most remarkable comeback album in the history of rock is "Rio Grande".

The eight-minute pop suite that closes side two serves notice that Brian Wilson is once again making ambitious, inventive and revolutionary pop

BRIAN WILSON

music, working in a style that is as "out there" in 1988 as "Good Vibrations" was in 1966. Brian is again redefining the pop song; besides being an unmistakably powerful masterpiece, "Rio Grande" is a classy reminder to the music world that there's more to recordmaking than 3 1/2 minute songs. It's "Rio Grande" that makes <u>Brian Wilson</u> not only a welcome fulfillment of musical dreams but a wonderful promise for the future.

As the Beach Boys, Brian's musical messengers, continue to take his California dream to their world of fans, the enduring and timeless quality of Brian's classic music proves itself every day.

And now, with <u>Brian Wilson</u>, Brian himself is offering new music to the ardent supporters who receive boundless joy from his spiritual sounds.

It is with great pride that Reprise and Sire Records welcome Brian not only to the record label but back to the creative world where he assumes his rightful place as one of the few legitimate musical geniuses of our time.

0688

David Leaf, who researched and wrote this press kit, is the author of the acclaimed Brian Wilson biography, <u>The Beach Boys & The California Myth</u>.

BRIAN WILSON

A Conversation with Brian...

(Brian Wilson took time out from the final mixing sessions of his album to discuss his artistic rebirth. The converation took place at Brian's Malibu home with David Leaf.)

DL: Brian, it's been 22 years since you produced Pet Sounds. Brian Wilson is your first major album since then, and it's your first ever solo LP. How come you decided to make another record?

BRIAN: It's the right time, a good time to make a record. The music has got to surface eventually. I think we're all afraid of what's inside of us and all our memories. That stuff got in the way, but you become more at peace with yourself. You have a handle on all the bad things that happened to you in your life. You say to yourself, "There's no way to get over this," but somehow, you do anyway. I'm driven by my ego and my love for music. You gotta get it out. To me, the highest thing in the world is to make music.

DL: So last spring, you began to work on your record?

BRIAN: After over a year of intense soul-searching and conversations with Dr. Landy, I decided to go ahead and try a solo album. I only had two conditions. The first was that he would be executive producer and fight the

business battles for me. And I said, "If I can do it at my pace, I'll make an album." So we proceeded to choose, from songs that I had written over the past five years. There were about a hundred, and we picked the best of the crop.

DL: You've spent almost a year making this record. That's the longest it's ever taken you to do an album. Is there a reason for that?

BRIAN: Yeah. About a year, a long time. The problem was that it took some time to get rolling on the vocals. The backgrounds were pretty good, but the leads, I had to keep doing them over. I was having trouble with my voice, but I found a great voice coach, who helped me out a little bit.

DL: Was the problem that you hadn't sung much in recent years?

BRIAN: Yeah. You know, I wasn't singing much. My voice is basically a falsetto kind of voice, and when I try to sing in legitimate voice, I become self-critical of my voice, you know? A lot of people said, "Brian, great vocals." But I'm essentially a falsetto singer.

DL: Everybody who has heard the rough mixes of the album, whether they're big fans of yours or just music lovers, has really loved it. How do you feel people are going to react to it?

BRIAN: I think with positivity, real positive feelings. Good sound, good lyrics, good vocals. I think people are gonna love it.

DL: When one sits down to create, it takes a lot of ego...

BRIAN: It sure does. Isn't ego another word for survival?

DL: I don't mean that kind of ego. I mean the ego that says that what I'm doing is so good that the world should pay attention. Do you have to pump yourself up like that?

BRIAN: Well, you gotta go by your track record. If you made good records in the '60s, then you're going to have to tell yourself, "I'm a good recordmaker." So you go on your past credentials, your past history.

DL: But when you were starting out in 1961, you didn't have a track record. Where did you get the confidence and ego to do it back then?

BRIAN: Phil Spector.

DL: He inspired you?

BRIAN: Yeah. I used to listen to Spector a lot.

DL: While you haven't been making many records in the last few years, there's been a technological revolution with emulators and digital recording and all sorts of amazing electronic hardware. What was it like adjusting to the new machines?

BRIAN: It was fun, a learning experience.

DL: In a sense, the machines today can do what you were trying to do in 1966 on your own. Does it make it easier for you?

BRIAN: Yeah, and it makes it faster, speeds up the process a little bit. We did this album differently than I used to. I used to get a group of people out there in the studio and produce the band live. Now, everything's done on synthesizers. I played most of this album, but now and then, we'd call in musicians for specific parts.

BRIAN WILSON

DL: Comparing the early tracks recorded for the album with the later material, it's clear how much stronger and confident you sound. Does that make you happy?

BRIAN: A little bit. It pumps up a lot of good confidence inside of me. It's very difficult at times to work in the studio under the guise of Brian Wilson, and the idea that I don't want to fail. I think this album is way better than Pet Sounds.

DL: Really?

BRIAN: Well, Pet Sounds is more artistic, but this one's more commercial.

DL: You've called Pet Sounds your love album. Is there one word to describe this record?

BRIAN: Happy.

DL: And that reflects the way you're feeling?

BRIAN: Yeah.

DL: In the past, you used the Beach Boys as a vocal instrument. Now, you're doing all the vocals yourself. Is that comfortable for you?

BRIAN: I could always sing high or low, but my basic forte is high voices. All the voices are me.

DL: The world has been waiting a long time for a Brian Wilson solo album. When people hear it, do you think they'll feel it was worth the wait?

BRIAN: Yeah. I think so. They'll just feel a new vibration from me.

DL: Is it a better feeling to create for just Brian Wilson and not other people?

BRIAN: Yeah, it's more centered, more right there, like it's being done for me at the time, so I can center with it. I can get centered with my album, put myself right in the middle. It's a good feeling.

DL: When you're finally holding the album in your hands and it says Brian Wilson, how do you think it will feel?

BRIAN: It will be like a baby that I had.

DL: And is it more your baby because it says "Brian Wilson" and not "The Beach Boys?"

BRIAN: Yeah, it's a personal baby. That's a good way to look at it.

DL: Who do you think this album will appeal to?

BRIAN: I like to write for young people, 'cause they understand what I'm saying in my music, understand where I'm coming from. But, I think this album should appeal to people in their twenties, thirties and forties.

DL: Do you think people will hear your album and say, "That's a great piece of art, and it's not like anything he's ever done before?"

BRIAN: Maybe people will think it's not a great piece of art but a commercial piece of art. An artist... the ability to put on canvas how you feel, like the "Mona Lisa." What an example of what a person felt like, created a feeling, a smile, a face. That soul. It makes you wonder. Is she smiling? What's she thinking? A subtle feeling. As an artist, you don't know if you're going to be able to get it out or on paper. It's very subtle. It can be done in every day life. You don't have to be in a studio making music, but that is a high point of a person's life, to go into the studio and record. To make music is the high point of my life. I value that more than sex.

DL: Do you feel that as you've grown older and grown up that your writing style has changed?

BRIAN: I write more about ideas, now. Before, I wrote about tangible kinds of things; now, I'm writing about ideas, love songs again. I'm back to love songs: "Melt Away" and "Love and Mercy" and "One For The Boys" and "There's So Many." There are four or five love songs on the album.

DL: Does that come out of all the love you feel for the world?

BRIAN: Yeah, it does. A lot of love went into the making of this record.

DL: Is there any way you could explain how you write a song.

BRIAN: Yeah. You just sit down and start playing around and come up with ideas. I'll be sitting there and I'll think (sings: "ba, ba, ba, ba, ba"). Then, I'll think, wait a minute, do that again, try this and that. Then, you start a pattern going, and all of a sudden, you've got a melody. All of a sudden, you start getting lyrics.

DL: So you're looking for a melody line first?

BRIAN: First a bag, then a melody line, then lyrics.

DL: What do you mean by "a bag?"

BRIAN: Rhythm and chords. My songwriting cycles are natural. When I get ready to go into a songwriting period, I feel that if I go to the piano and sit there long enough, something's gonna happen, my hands are gonna be lifted up by God and plopped down on the keys. It's that automatic.

DL: When you write a song, do you know whether it's a hit right away?

BRIAN WILSON

BRIAN: I have a basic gut response to the song that makes me feel positive that it might make it.

DL: Of the songs you've written recently, which ones have given you that feeling?

BRIAN: "Love and Mercy," "Walkin' The Line" and "Nightime."

DL: When do you like to write best?

BRIAN: At night. Real peaceful.

DL: When you write, are you inspired by what you see, like the view of the ocean we have from you living room?

BRIAN: No. It all comes from inside.

DL: Are you always writing a song in your head?

BRIAN: Not always. Whenever I go through my songwriting cycles, I follow through with it, keep going with it 'cause I've got something happening.

DL: Is it frustrating to have the music in your head and you can't get it out?

BRIAN: It's a burden sometimes. Yeah, it is.

DL: What's the best way to deal with it?

BRIAN: I get into it. "Love and Mercy" is an example of that. Of feeling a bag in my head, of carrying it around for a while and finally getting it out.

DL: You're an autobiographical songwriter?

BRIAN WILSON

BRIAN: Yeah. "Love and Mercy" and "Melt Away" are the two philosophical records that I made on this album.

DL: "Love and Mercy" is what I call a diary song. Like "Busy Doin' Nothin'" on <u>Friends</u>, "Love and Mercy" gives you an idea of what it's like to spend some time with Brian Wilson. Do you remember when you got the idea for that?

BRIAN: I was in my piano room, and I was playing "What The World Needs Now, Is Love, Sweet Love," and I just went into my own song. I worked very hard to get out of me what was in my heart on that one. I called up Dr. Landy and we worked on the lyrics together. I was going for a spiritual, semi-Beach Boy kind of background sound, but more of a Brian Wilson lead vocal thing. "Love and Mercy" is a real positive vibe; it really is.

DL: Your music has always spread a really happy vibe to the world.

BRIAN: Yes, it has. It has. Some of it's sad. "Caroline No" from <u>Pet Sounds</u> was a sad song. But I'm a positive kind of artist. I see my whole career as a stab at trying to get across some messages to people. My first and foremost message of all is to bring out love, is to bring love to people. Then, comes exhilirating music that makes people feel alive, rock 'n' roll.

DL: You consider your music to be spiritual don't you?

BRIAN: The spirituality of my music is explained by the fact that if you don't take it upon yourself to create something, no one will. If you don't take that attitude, who's gonna take it? That's why I say the spiritualness of my music comes and goes. Some of my songs are very spiritual, like "The

Warmth of the Sun" from the early Beach Boys days. And "Love and Mercy" is very spiritual. Maybe love and spirituality are about the same. How can you really differentiate love and spirituality?

DL: You seem very inspired these days. Is the attention of a hit record what you need to be inspired to keep doing it?

BRIAN: People should realize that there's even more than just this solo album that I've got in me. I worked hard, did the best for you all; it's something that you do out of love.

DL: When you know people are listening, do you just want to give them more? Does that work for you?

BRIAN: Yeah. I plan it like this. I say, "If there is a listening need, then there is an artistic supply." In other words, if there is a need, then the art must be created for that need. It's a beautiful thing. Very spiritual. Music is all over the place.

DL: In 1970, you made a terrific record called "This Whole World"...

BRIAN: (sings a verse of "This Whole World") Yeah, I remember that song.

DL: But the world didn't pick up on it. What happens when you do your job as an artist but the world doesn't do their job and get your message. Is that discouraging?

BRIAN: All that is trial and error. You put the record out and it bombs. Who do you blame it on? Yourself or the public? Was the record not good enough or did the public feel too fickle to buy your record? Neither. It's bad karma.

DL: Getting back to the songs on your album...what can you tell me about

BRIAN WILSON

"Nighttime?"

BRIAN: The process of twilight, dusk turning into total darkness has always fascinated me. All of my life. I've always been a night person, never did like the daytime, which signifies work time.

DL: What do you like to do at night?

BRIAN: I like to bowl, watch MTV, stay current with what's going on on TV. I watch MTV for entertainment purposes, and also because I want to get a feel for just how warm this world is, like the way the music has warmth and coldness too. Because MTV, new wave, is both warm and cold. The lyrics are warm, they talk about love, and the other is like coldness, one fleeting image to another. And it's all tied together with warm and cold.

DL: Do you feel your music is real warm?

BRIAN: Some of it.

DL: What's the warmest thing you've ever done?

BRIAN: Probably "Surfer Girl."

DL: Of everything on the album, "Melt Away" is one of the warmest.

BRIAN: That's a spiritual sound. How many different ways can you say "Merry Christmas?" But if you try, you can find a new way to do it. What Gene and I wanted to do on "Melt Away" was find a new way to say that "you make my blues fade away." That theme in music has been done so many times, it's ridiculous; but there are new and innovative ways to say that, and I think we said it in this song.

DL: You told me that "Melt Away" also came right from your life.

BRIAN WILSON

BRIAN: It's about the identity crisis I have in my life---the way I see myself and the "me" that everybody thinks I am. You go through some hassles over that some times. I might feel one thing inside, but you get feedback from people that you're not that way. It's a strange trip; it really is.

DL: Do you remember what you were feeling when you wrote "Melt Away?" You sing, "the world's not waiting just for me, the world don't care what I can be." Do you believe that?

BRIAN: Yeah. Absolutely. I've been through it. I know. I lived it.

DL: "Baby Let Your Hair Grow Long" also sounds like it was written with a strong point-of-view.

BRIAN: It is, of course, a sexual song, a song about sexual ideas. At first, when I wrote the melody, I thought maybe it should be a love song. 'Cause it started sounding like a love song to me. And I tried a working lyric that had a lot to do with love and affection and that kind of thing. But I didn't like it. Most of the lyrics were romantic, but then I put in a couple of sexual lines. And then I said, "Wait a minute. Let's get rid of some of the love aspects, the romantic aspects of this song, and put in more sexual lyrics."

DL: When I first heard "Baby...", I thought of the end of <u>Pet Sounds</u> when you sing "Where did your long hair go?" It's kind of like you're singing to that same thing. Do you feel that at all, or is it just my imagination?

BRIAN: No, it's still the same mood. The mood is sexual.

DL: I thought that the lyrics were sung to yourself.

BRIAN: It's just the opposite; it's for others.

DL: The line, "There's gotta be something you're living for, you've got to try a little more," sounds to me like you're giving yourself a pep talk.

BRIAN: It's a pep talk, but not to myself. It's like when girls whack their hair off short, and they don't give a shit. Sometimes, if you prompt a girl, prompt someone to hit the road and get on the stick and let your hair grow long and try harder. Instead of saying "go out and exercise and eat health foods and all that stuff," and all the messages that most of the people missed. That's one song in itself; another song is called "Poor Old Body." But if you're just saying, "You've got to try a little more," that generally means you've got to get your head a little more into success, orient yourself towards more success in your mind. A mental success mechanism. That's what I meant by "you've got to try a little more."

DL: Does long hair symbolize something to you?
BRIAN: It exemplifies beauty in a girl.

DL: So you're saying...
BRIAN: Make yourself beautiful again.

DL: The whole musical feeling of "Baby..." makes me think it could have fit nicely onto Pet Sounds.
Brian: That could have been on Pet Sounds because it's a classic piece of art, a work of art that I worked on for many months, changing it and molding it and shaping it and reshaping it and fine-tuning it, to get the sound I like. I came into the studio with the attitude that I could do it. I never felt any less than perfect. So when I go into the studio, I know I'm shaping something together.

DL: How did you produce "There's So Many?" When you sing, "The planets are spinning around," you give the listener the feeling that the planets really are spinning around.

BRIAN: There are lines that come out of me. "There's So Many" has more love appeal than anything else on the album. It's like a dive into a voice sound, into an arrangement. That line is subtle inference that astrology affects our lives. There's gotta be 15 or 16 voices on there. I really thickened it up, made it real thick and fat, which, I understand a lot of people like that "fat" sound.

DL: Was this really a spiritual song for you?

BRIAN: Very much so, especially the harmonies in (sings) "Planets are spinning around." Probably the most spiritual part of the whole album. It just had a vibration to it, you know? It was like, "Whew." I didn't know where it was coming from. I listened to it, and I (felt) "What!?"

DL: Does that ever scare you, that those things come through you like that?

BRIAN: No. A creator is never afraid of what he creates. Never. Because it's too natural. A person who creates a vibration is never afraid of it, because it's just natural. Do you think a bee is afraid of a flower? No.

DL: What about the astrological aspect of "There's So Many"?

BRIAN: Michael Bernard, who is the greatest programmer I ever met, brought a telescope to the studio one night, and I looked at Jupiter, and I saw the craters on the moon. But just the idea of looking through a telescope, thinking about the planets and do they really have an affect on our minds? And do they really affect the way people react to each other and interact with each other? Is there some kind of a reaction between people that has something to do with planets in the sky? A lot of people feel this is true.

DL: Another song on the album is "Walkin' The Line." Do you walk the line?
BRIAN: Yeah, every day. The lyrics are all about me, how I'm always walking over thin ice, could fall through at any minute. I tread lightly on everything I do, walk the line so to speak. Not all the time, but it is one of my sub-theme songs of my whole life. When I wrote that, I was at the piano, and I was remembering an old bass line that I had written, a left hand. And I said to myself, "I want to record a song that has bass sounds like a '60s record but has an '80s feeling to it, an '80s vibration. So I took that old bass line that I had never finished and incorporated it into a new kind of sound. It was all in remembering the feeling, the spirit I had when I wrote the bass line a long time ago. I always felt good about that left hand, a good vibration about it.

DL: When you walk the line in your life, have you ever crossed onto the wrong side of the line?
BRIAN: Sure. I've fallen through a lot of times. Now, I'm back on my feet. You know, it's not a serious song.

DL: "Little Children" is also a fun song, kind of a "wall of sound" old-style ditty. What was there about kids that inspired that one?
BRIAN: There is no responsibility when you're a kid, and I admire the freedom from responsibility that kids have. I'm jealous of it. That track was done as an attempt to make people feel younger. (Imitates the sound of the record.) I feel that the way it was put together, if you're 60, it

should make you feel 40. When I hear it, I feel a lot younger, about 20. You can have a child in you that's playful and young.

DL: Do you wish you were a kid again?
BRIAN: Oh yeah, I think about that all the time. I'd like to be 17 again, if I could.

DL: "One For The Boys" has a very melancholy feel to it.
BRIAN: That is a love song that has feminine characteristics. It's the feminine side of me.

DL: "Let It Shine" was done with Jeff Lynne. What was it like working with somebody who was so influenced by you?
BRIAN: I thought it might be too sterile, but as we did it in the studio, I said, "You know, Jeff, this is coming out real good."

DL: "Poor Old Body To Move" was a song you worked on with Lindsey Buckingham, somebody else who is a big fan of yours. You obviously think exercise is important.
BRIAN: It's the most important thing in the world if you want to have a brain to think with.

DL: What's "Meet Me In My Dreams Tonight" about?
BRIAN: It's about a guy and a girl who love each other on a certain level that's higher than real life. A fantasy song. We wanted to get the sound like "Sweet Talkin' Guy," that kind of '60s feeling in a record in the '80s.

DL: Everybody who has heard "Rio Grande" is just blown away by it.

BRIAN WILSON

BRIAN: That was a labor of love, and that's probably the best thing on the whole album. It's taken the longest to do, and we tried to pull it together so that it makes sense. So that people can hear it and it will flow naturally from one thing to another. Real hard to do at first.

DL: How did you decide to even try a song like that?

BRIAN: Lenny Waronker thought I could do it, and it looks like Lenny was right.

DL: Were you reluctant to do that kind of thing at first?

BRIAN: Yes, I was. But Andy Paley helped me out a little bit with songs and gave me a new direction in it.

DL: What exactly did Andy do?

BRIAN: Andy Paley conceptualized lyrically what was happening. He did a little more of the lyrics than I did; but I did a little more music. The two were a perfect marriage.

DL: When Lenny came to you and said he didn't want you to write another song, he wanted you to do a piece of music, that must have seemed pretty strange. Don't record company presidents usually tell you to write more hits?

BRIAN: Yeah, but he figured that there was one left in me, that there was a suite, a rock opera that I could do. And we did it.

DL: Lenny's a big fan of the kind of stuff you did in `66 and `67, "Heroes and Villains" and "Cabin Essence." Those songs have lots of different sections; they were written in pieces like "Rio Grande". Did Lenny have to work hard to convince you to work in that style again?

BRIAN: Yeah. He wanted me to get a little bit into that kind of _Smile_ bag, and I did. Some of it took on characteristics of the _Smile_ album, but that's all, just characteristics. It wasn't directly influenced by _Smile_, just the vibes of it, the basic feeling of it.

DL: It's been a long time since you've worked that way. Was it hard for you to do "Rio Grande"?

BRIAN: As I remember, at first, it was uncomfortable for me.

DL: You just did the final mix on "Rio Grande" yesterday. Was it very satisfying to finish it?

BRIAN: Yeah. It completes a musical thought in my head. It makes something complete (bangs on the table for emphasis). And the completion of the project is the satisfaction of knowing that you've done it; you've gone through it and you did it.

DL: "Rio Grande" sounds to me like it could be a ride at Disneyland.

BRIAN: That would be great.

DL: What would you like people to feel when they hear "Rio Grande?"

BRIAN: I would like a person to feel joy.

DL: There are six or seven different sections to the song. What's your favorite part?

BRIAN: I personally like the "Take Me Home" section.

DL: Is that at all autobiographical?

BRIAN: It's a song that expresses the need to be.

DL: How did you come up with the "Rain Dance" section? You were talking before about Smile, and it's kind of like...

BRIAN: The "Rain Dance?" That was something I didn't like. That's the only part I really didn't like as much. The mood of the "Rain Dance" is too scary.

DL: But it fits in with the rest and completes the suite?
BRIAN: Yes.

DL: One of the things you're known for is your use of unusual instruments...

BRIAN: First of all, I'm a genius at music, at instruments. I could play a piano and make it happen without anything else. I could make the groove to a point where we wouldn't need anything else. Although records need more than piano, I could do it. A piano and a voice, that would be perfect.

DL: This album represents a whole new kind of record-making for you. Do you like modern recording studios?

BRIAN: Yeah. Multi-tracking is much better. The track on "Baby Let Your Hair Grow Long" was something you couldn't have done back in the '60s without screwing up.

DL: On "Baby..." you used an electric saw.
BRIAN: I'm known for a theremin or something weird. That saw is a little like a theremin.

DL: You're playing a lot of different instruments on emulators. Instead of working with a musician, you're working with a machine. What was that like?
BRIAN: It saved time, and it made me more able to play it myself, to make

it sound more rhythmically right. There are a lot of reasons I like working with emulators rather than live musicians.

DL: Back in the sixties, didn't the studio musicians you worked with give you lots of positive feedback, some good ideas? Don't you miss that?
BRIAN: No, because it all rests in my head. That's where my music is.

DL: What are your favorite musical touches on the album?
BRIAN: I liked the sampled saxophone on "Walking the Line." On "Love and Mercy," I cut the track in Hawaii, cut the background track in Honolulu. It had such a good left-hand sound; you know what I mean? It had a good vibe to it.

DL: Somebody once said you had the best left hand in the business.
BRIAN: That's not true.

DL: Who's got a better one?
BRIAN: Motown.

DL: Any other instrumental parts you especially liked?
BRIAN: In "Baby, Let Your Hair Grow Long," the oboe, and the background voices in the verse. In "Nighttime," the part that drones. I thought that was really good.

DL: As an artist, it's been quite a while since you made a big statement. What took so long?
BRIAN: It's the right time. I had to get my head and my health together first. I had to take care of basics. In my therapy, I've been learning to

BRIAN WILSON

be less afraid, more confident and more independent. I had to get in shape first before I could make another creative statement. I'm pretty positive about this record. I think it's a spiritual album; I think it's gonna be a hit. I really do.

DL: Is there one central theme that unites this record with your previous work?

BRIAN: Love is the theme of my whole album.

DL: Because this is the first Brian Wilson album, do you feel like you're beginning a new career?

BRIAN: Yeah. For sure. This is my new album. This is the first time I've ever had an album. Twenty six years being in the business, that's a lot of years.

DL: What does it feel like to have a solo record?

BRIAN: It feels good. It feels like an expansive mood. (I'm) moving forward. You're doing something; you're initiating something. It's a good feeling.

DL: Are you concerned about the way it'll be received?

BRIAN: I think so. It's not like forcing somebody to like your stuff. It's just an easygoing album that I think will and should be well-received.

DL: The world has an image of you...

BRIAN: Yeah, you and I were talking about that dilemma between that image the world has of you and you have of yourself. What does the world think of me?

DL: I think you know the legend. What do you see as the man behind legend

BRIAN WILSON

opposed to the way the world sees you?

BRIAN: A much more creative person than the legend. Somebody with many more personal ideas floating around in his head than any person that considers me a legend would be able to conceive of.

DL: What kind of ideas do you have inside that you're getting ready to share with the world?
BRIAN: Love and my voice. I can only give my voice.

DL: People have this picture of Brian Wilson as a reclusive genius who doesn't get around in the world very much. Did that bother you?
BRIAN: It bothered me a little bit.

DL: Is it hard to live up to people's expectations of you?
BRIAN: It's pretty hard. It's interesting to do. It keeps you on your toes. It keeps you going.

DL: When people buy this album, it'll be part because of the legend and part because of the man. Which do you like better?
BRIAN: The man.

DL: Is that what really comes through on Brian Wilson?
BRIAN: Pretty much, yeah. I want to present a new image to the world. Here I am. This is the new solo album.

DL: You're not a choir boy anymore.
BRIAN: That's the part of the image people have of me that's hard to accept.
'Cause I changed my image, but people still hang on to that old image.
DL: You changed it a long time ago, back in 1966?

BRIAN: Yeah.

DL: Do you think the world is finally gonna catch up to you?

BRIAN: I don't know. I hope so. I just hope that I get a fair chance to sell records.

DL: But for an artist, isn't there a lot of satisfaction that you get just in the creating?

BRIAN: Yeah, that's true. That's something I thought about. And you know, when you work with music, there's a satisfaction that goes along with just making the record, rather than wondering whether it's gonna sell.

DL: Are you real satisfied with the record you've made?

BRIAN: Yeah. Very.

DL: Do you think you'll be more satisfied with the next one?

BRIAN: Yeah, I might. If I'm not careful, I might wind up getting my mind blown (laughs). What I'm trying to say is that I could blow my own mind with music.

DL: Is that what happened the last time?

BRIAN: Yeah.

DL: So you needed time to recover from that?

BRIAN: Yeah. It blew my mind to make all that music. It just did.

DL: "Rio Grande" is kind of walking down that road again.

BRIAN: Yeah. Yeah.

DL: Is that scary?

BRIAN WILSON

BRIAN: No, I've been there.

DL: Are you ready for it?
BRIAN: Yeah. Sure. If you are (laughs).

DL: In the '60s, our records had a major impact on the business. Will the Brian Wilson album affect the music industry?
BRIAN: It will bring back love to the record industry.

DL: You got quite an ovation at the Rock & Roll Hall of Fame induction ceremonies this year.
BRIAN: It's a good feeling to get an award. I made a speech...talked about the chronology of the Beach Boys...how music is something that touched people, and that we all share that feeling in this room, that feeling of music...you're just a human being, but God writes it through you.

DL: You said that "music is the voice of God."
BRIAN: I believe it. Yes. Absolutely.

DL: That's quite a responsibility isn't it?
BRIAN: It is, but you can immerse in it.

DL: Is it hard for you to live up to the "gifts" God's given you?
BRIAN: No. Not anymore. It used to be. I went through a few trips of hell about that, not being able to handle those things; but I've been there so many times that I'm getting good at going there and getting those places together. Regardless if it's a lost feeling or a threatened feeling, feeling threatened or feeling lost, it's just one of those things.
DL: When everybody hears the new record, they're going to want to come and

see you in person. Any plans for a tour?

BRIAN: Absolutely. I have to get an act together.

DL: Besides the new album, any songs from the past that you would like to perform?

BRIAN: Yeah, a couple of Beach Boys songs, "Sloop John B.," "Help Me Rhonda" and "Surfer Girl." I gotta put a band together, a band similar to the Beach Boys. I'm looking for guys that can learn fast. I gotta teach these guys how do do it. It's like walking up a hill again.

DL: Besides music, what's on your mind these days, what's interesting you?

BRIAN: I follow athletics a lot. I try to keep in touch with them, but it's very hard 'cause I'm always on the run, and I don't have time to watch TV too much. I like basketball. I've always liked basketball. I think it's a cool game. Just the thought of somebody moving around, throwing a ball, jumping in the air is kind of exciting. Athletics have always inspired me.

DL: One of your newer hobbies is going to the race track. What do you like about watching the horses?

BRIAN: I like it all. I like to see them run, and I like to see the people just sitting around. Real relaxing.

DL: Are you a big bettor?

BRIAN: No. I only bet two bucks at a time?

DL: When people hear the record, they'll wonder what your life is like. What's a typical day for Brian Wilson?

BRIAN WILSON

BRIAN: Exercise, watching my calories. Basically doing my job, which is making music. Lately, a typical day has been to go to the studio, and absorb all the pressure that I can and keep myself cool. And make good music for people, you know? Make music that will make people happy, 'cause that's what makes me happy. It does. It really does.

DL: Your album will be out soon. What are you thinking about?

BRIAN: I think it's the right time for me to emerge. I should definitely put my soul on the line for people and see how far I can take my music. Music goes forever.

DL: And that's your job?

BRIAN: Exactly.

DL: One last question. Is there anything you want to say to the people who won't get a chance to talk with you?

BRIAN: I hope that everybody realizes how hard it was for us to make this album and how much it means for us to make music for people. So I hope they like it as much as we liked making it.

BRIAN WILSON

The Making of the Album

There's an old saying that goes: "Nobody wants to hear about the labor pains, they just want to see the baby." But when an album as important as <u>Brian Wilson</u> comes out, once you've heard "the baby," you'll want to know how it came to be.

As the album's executive producer Dr. Eugene Landy explains, the record's genesis dates back to late 1983 "when Brian and I started writing. The first songs were therapeutic, but very quickly, we were doing real writing together. In 1984, Brian worked on the last Beach Boys album, but it became clear that the Beach Boys didn't appreciate his gift nor were they able to see that he was back and once again able to take over. When they hired Steve Levine as producer, Brian and I talked it over and decided that it was time for him to pursue his solo career and make a solo album."

Flashforward to January, 1987. Sire President Seymour Stein recalls meeting Brian. "We needed somebody to introduce Jerry Leiber and Mike Stoller at the 2nd annual Rock and Roll Hall of Fame dinner. At a directors meeting, I suggested that we ask Brian Wilson. Everyone was thrilled by that prospect, because Brian just isn't seen on stage very much."

Sire Records · 75 Rockefeller Plaza · 20th Floor · New York, New York · 10019 · (212) 484-6870
Reprise Records, Inc. · 3300 Warner Boulevard · Burbank, California · 91510 · (818) 953-3223

BRIAN WILSON

"Brian accepted," Seymour continues, and that night, "by coincidence, Brian and I gave our speeches back-to-back." As Seymour watched from the wings, Brian went out to induct Leiber & Stoller. Brian began by singing a verse of "On Broadway," a moving acapella vocal that brought tears to the eyes of industry veterans and rock superstars in attendance...an incredibly poignant moment and clearly one of the legitimate highlights of the superstar-studded night.

But more than that, Brian's heartwarming appearance engendered some serious thinking, particularly from Seymour Stein, who was so determined to make an impression on Brian that he called Andy Paley (once a Sire Records artist and friend) in London for advice. "Andy fed me a bunch of lines, told me what songs to tell Brian I liked, not my obvious favorites like 'God Only Knows' but real obscure ones like 'Male Ego' (written by Brian and Dr. Landy a few years earlier), and 'Solar System.'"

Intrigued that anybody in the room had even heard of those songs, Brian invited Seymour to sit down; Seymour's "shanghai" worked, but only because they discovered a common ground---they both know and love songs of every imaginable vintage. A new friendship was born.

That same evening, another member of the audience, Warner Brothers president Lenny Waronker, allowed a long dormant fantasy to be reactivated. "Brian's speech was so wonderfully sweet," Lenny recalls. "I remember thinking, 'My god, maybe there can be more stuff like he used to do...maybe he should do a record. It was clear that Brian was on the way back; this wasn't the Brian Wilson of the 'Brian's Back' hype of 1976."

BRIAN WILSON

Lenny said nothing to anybody about his reverie, just sat back and fondly remembered the long ago time "when I was just starting out as a producer, and Brian was working with my good friend Van Dyke Parks. I loved the things they were working on, like 'Heroes and Villains' and 'Cabin Essence.' I had never forgotten how great that music was, or how much I loved 'Cool, Cool Water,' another incredible piece of music" Brian had recorded when the Beach Boys were signed to Brother/Reprise in 1970.

"Flying back from the Hall of Fame dinner, I was thinking how wonderful it would be if Brian could do a record, and he could do a bunch of things like 'Cool, Cool Water,' and we'd get 'em played on all those wave stations, a new age record with Brian Wilson."

In the darkened cabin, Lenny looked out the window and then towards the aisle, where he was startled to see Brian Wilson sitting there, headphones in place, playing his portable Casio. Lenny smiled to himself and turned away not wanting to interrupt Brian.

"When I got back to L.A.," Lenny continues, "Seymour called and said, in passing, that he was thinking of signing Brian. I said, 'Great! That's a brilliant idea. As a matter of fact, I've been thinking about the same thing.' And I told Seymour what I thought, about how I wanted to make a record filled with 'Cool, Cool Water' type of tracks. And Seymour said, 'Why don't we do half songs and half' what I call 'arts and crafts.'

"That was the beginning. Seymour, of course, moves much quicker than I do. He picked up the ball and made a deal."

BRIAN WILSON

In December of '86, Brian made his most impressive public appearances to date, singing three songs (and getting two standing ovations) at the National Academy of Songwriters annual salute, and when the Beach Boys celebrated their 25th anniversary with a Hawaiian TV special, Brian topped off the show with a brand new anthem, "The Spirit of Rock 'n' Roll."

So by the time the Hall of Fame dinner invitation came in, Brian's creative resurgence was well under way. Plenty of songs were on tape; Brian was finally ready to make his first solo album.

But while Brian's creative confidence had been restored, he was concerned that he would have a tough time dealing with the creative and business aspects of a solo career, so when Dr. Landy suggested that Brian make a solo album, he insisted that Dr. Landy produce it with him. Dr. Landy agreed to be the executive producer. As Brian explained it, Dr. Landy would oversee all the social and business aspects which would allow Brian to concentrate on the musical elements of producing. They also agreed that they would confer with each other and agree on all aspects of the album.

So the night of the Hall of Fame dinner, Seymour Stein, Dr. Eugene Landy and Brian Wilson made a deal. Next step---assemble a studio team. Synthesizer programmer Michael Bernard, discovered by Brian's musical assistant Andy Dean, was first on board. Sire assigned Andy Paley to be its

A&R man on the project, and after a number of false starts, engineer Mark Linett took over the board. Working on a regular basis with this team, the Brian lead studio quartet put down a solid dozen songs in April and May of 1987.

BRIAN WILSON

Michael Bernard describes a typical day in the studio. "Brian would come in, say 'Today, we're recording 'Nighttime.' He already had in his head the whole picture of what it was going to be like, and he would put down the different sounds. The way he would go about layering things, his choice of sounds and instrument was different from what I was used to, but it was really interesting to watch him work. Most people put down drums, bass and chords first, but Brian might go from the drums to horns to strings to a lead vocal. One of the first sounds he asked me for was a nuclear explosion to put on the beginning of 'Doin' Time on Planet Earth.'"

Brian, who was really a novice in synthesizer programming, found an able teacher in Bernard. "I explained to him what could be done, and he got the idea, thought it was neat that you could get any sound you wanted. Just to get him familiar with the synthesizer, I showed him how to do certain things. He has a DX-7 at home, so he was aware of some of the capabilities of the equipment, but I went through my sound library to give him the ideas of the possibilities of it. And as we worked more and more, and he became more familiar with what the sampler could do and what sounds were available, he would go home thinking about those sounds and come in and say, 'Let's start off with that saxophone sound we had a week ago.'"

Michael Bernard points out that Brian took the lead. "Brian always had an idea of what he wanted for layering. Once in a while, he would get to a point where he would say, 'I've got another line; I want you to come up with an interesting sounding patch on the keyboard.' And I would go on my own and try to figure out what might work that Brian would like. That's where it became difficult because sometimes he would be conventional and other times he would want off-the-wall sounds. Whatever he picked, it came out great."

BRIAN WILSON

Brian's ability to absorb the new technology was incredibly quick, Bernard notes. "As I was showing him some sounds, he'd go 'Wait a minute.' He would hear a line in his head that went with that sound, so he wanted to put that line down on tape right away."

And Brian's legendary love of new sounds found new flower in the infinite library of the sampler. "On 'There's So Many,' the part where Brian sings 'The planets are spinning around.' He asked me 'What kind of sound could we put in there to give you that feeling that the planets really are spinning around?' We came up with this light chime which sounds almost like a windchime; it gives a motion effect to the song when you hear it."

And naturally, from the man who ended his classic Pet Sounds album with barking dogs and a train, non-musical sounds played an important role in this record as Michael Bernard explains. "He really liked the sound effects that I could get out of the equipment. On 'Nighttime,' for example, he said 'Do you have any sounds that sound like night?' I played him the crickets, which he loved and then the frog croaking which he put in. In general, he would ask for sounds that were visual."

Because Brian had the overview of how he wanted each song to sound, Bernard continues, "usually, Brian would work out his whole thing on tape, and then he would turn around and ask what we thought or ask me to put in a certain kind of sound. In the process, if I got an idea, I could suggest it to him. He was open. The general atmosphere was great. If anybody had an idea...none of that was stifled."

By the late spring of 1987, most of the album had been cut, but, as Dr. Landy recalls, Brian wasn't satisfied. Because Brian wanted the record to sound modern, he and Dr. Landy decided to bring in a co-producer, somebody who, as Lenny Waronker put it, "could take what Brian had done to the next level."

Everybody agreed that the person for the job was Russ Titelman, the Grammy Award winning producer who had once worked with Brian in 1965 on "Guess I'm Dumb," Brian's best non-Beach Boys production and an important record in that it was foreshadowing of the sound that Brian would use the next year on Pet Sounds.

The scene changed from west to east---New York City, June, 1987. Russ Titelman explains the change in Brian Wilson. "When I had worked with him in '65, he was completely in control, a creative cornucopia, exploding with all music, all the time. He still has all of the talent, but he needs a little guidance. He used to be a benevolent dictator in the studio; now, his ideas are great, but he needs somebody to help organize those ideas."

Russ points out that "in the studio, I was just trying to lead him in a direction. For instance, when we did 'There's So Many,' I said to him, 'Do your harmony thing on this.' And he went into the studio and did it. That's how we worked together. My job was to egg him on, make him do stuff that maybe he wouldn't have done, hope we shared the same taste. In that way, I was helpl, a catalyst."

That's not to say that there weren't difficult moments in the collaboration. Brian and Dr. Landy hired me, and I did what I had to do. I figured, 'I'll be strong and do my job, and if they don't like it, they can fire me.' We all know from the end product of what Brian did in the 'old days' that he's a genius. So I wasn't going to allow anybody except Brian to tell me what to do. I'm singleminded when I get into the studio. When we're working, I don't really care about personalities. I just want to get the best record. In certain ways, I don't really care about how people feel. I was sensitive to Brian's quirkiness and to his feelings about certain things, but after a point, he knows what's good and he knows what to do. And I know what to do. We're both professionals. So if he was going off track, I would say 'This is no good.' I was very tough about what I thought, made no bones."

In June, during their first sessions for the album, Titelman recalls a burst of creative energy. "We did about four or five days of great work. In that first week, we finished 'There's So Many,' added a bridge and some great vocal stuff to 'Love and Mercy'...a tremendous amount of work in a few days. It was so exciting. Brian was 'on it.' Once he would get going, it was amazing. I'd say, 'What do you want to do now?' He'd say, 'Get me a horn sound.' And he'd play it on the emulator, and it would be really great. Or I'd say, 'Let's do the background vocals.' And he'd say, 'Give me eight tracks.' And he'd go out into the studio, and in twenty minutes, he would have all the backgrounds done. It was like the old days when you'd finish a whole record in one day."

In fact, Brian was on such a roll, Dr. Landy recalls, that "on weekends, while everybody else wanted to rest and enjoy New York City, Brian couldn't wait to get into the studio. Russ had gotten Brian up-to-date in the studio, and on Sundays, Brian wanted to use his new recording knowledge alone, without anybody around. So Brian went in with just the second engineer. On one Sunday, he cut 'One For The Boys' and on another, 'Walkin' The Line.'"

BRIAN WILSON

Like everybody involved in this record, Russ is a fan of Brian's Beach Boys work, and what he "loved most on those records was this beautiful counterpoint, Bach-like singing on 'God Only Knows.' So when we were doing 'Love and Mercy,' I said to Brian, 'Do 'God Only Knows' in here.' And he'd go out in the studio and off the cuff, off the top of his head, come up with these parts and lay 'em down. He would double 'em, and it would sound like the Beach Boys. Same thing happened on 'Melt Away.' I was always pushing him to do that; it's his signature. Once he got going, I tried to stay out of the way because he was just doing his stuff, as brilliant as ever."

What did Russ Titelman bring to the project? Dr. Eugene Landy explains, "Russ gave Brian a crash course in current studio technology, brought him from four track to forty-eight track. He contemporized what

Brian had done in L.A., made it work in today's terms, made Brian comfortable with the machines, so that by the time we left New York, Brian was able to continue the album at this new, higher level. Russ really contributed a tremendous amount to the artistic success of this album."

In putting Russ' work in perspective, Lenny Waronker believes that "Russ did a real good job of helping Brian realize the beauty of his music, helped it stand up. Brian hasn't done this in a long time, and he needed help with the technology. And where it needed some small fixing, Russ was able to show Brian how to do it in a simple way."

"What I remember most was what Russ said to me early on. I got a call one night from the studio. Russ was so excited. He just kept repeating, 'There's nothing to do here. It's all Brian. All I have to do is help him in a few areas, but it's his thing.' Russ sounded so thrilled, telling me that watching Brian work was like magic, a producer's dream."

When Lenny heard the results of all the hard work, "the idea that Brian was able to do this after so much time away was really shocking, beyond what anybody could expect. Brian hadn't been actively involved in the studio in many years, and he really just needed to get back in shape. By the end of the record, he was moving so quickly, like somebody on an exercise program who's progressing at a really rapid pace. The whole recordmaking thing came back to him. In some ways, he's similar to Prince in that he moves quickly."

And, to everybody's pleasure, as Lenny points out, "the songs are as if Brian picked up from Pet Sounds and the best of what followed Pet Sounds, and yet somehow, it sounds like a record that was made today."

Rejoicing in Brian's reawakened musical gifts, what probably surprised everybody most was Brian's lyric writing. Lenny Waronker: "We always knew that he wrote the greatest melodies and was a musical genius, but in fact, the lyrical ideas that he has are very, very good. I never realized that Brian was a real, classic songwriter who, given the chance, somehow comes up with these wonderful touching sounds that are bigger than your average song. And behind each one is some very deep thinking."

The emotional depth of Brian's music has always been one of its main attractions, and on the solo album, many of the lyrics come not just from his feelings but from the intellectual searching tht has been part of his recovery. Explaining how they originally collaborated lyrically, Dr. Landy recalls that "when we would write, Brian, Alexandra and I would sit around and have these extraordinary philosophical conversations during which Alexandra and I would find out what was on Brian's mind. He tends to be more ethereal than people comprehend, and Alexandra was able to take the broader aspects of our philosophy and bring them into concrete form lyrically. Alexandra was always able to express Brian's point of view, to help him say what he wanted to say and express his ideas coherently and poetically."

Alexandra Morgan remembers that writing with Brian is full of wonderful moments. "The three of us can be having this terrific discussion on life and love and the heavens above and suddenly, Brian will jump up and say, 'I've got to go to the piano.' And then he'll come back in ten or fifteen minutes with the sketch of the song. Like on 'There's So Many,' he had the melody and the line 'The planets are spinning around.' Eugene and I took it from there."

"Because I know Brian so well," Dr. Landy points out, "I am able to sharpen and bring into focus the lyrical images of his songs, so that the lyrics, while not necessarily written by Brian, accurately reflect his thoughts and feelings. For example, we often talk about fantasy, so it's natural to put that into 'There's So Many.'"

There was no typical songwriting session. "Sometimes," Dr. Landy notes, "Brian would call, ready to write, and he would say, 'Give me a title.' Then, he'd put together a rough lyric, and modem it over to me, and we'd go back and forth. Sometimes, we would write on an airplane, with two headphones hooked into a casio keyboard."

Russ Titelman was astounded by both the speed and quality of the lyric writing. "When we were finishing up recording 'Nighttime,' there was a lyric that wasn't perfect. I said to Brian, 'This is kind of weak.' So he thought for a second and came up with 'Downtown where the sun beats strong/eight hours is a little too long.' And in 'Melt away,' at the last minute, he came up with 'I feel just like an island/until I see you smilin.' If I said, 'I think those lines could be better or the vocals could be better,' Brian would do it on the spot, take ten or fifteen minutes. Always great stuff. Unbelievable."

The New York sojourn a success, Brian spent the rest of the summer polishing the tracks and vocls, and by September, had just about completed what looked like a very good first solo album.

It was at this point that Lenny Waronker decided to make his presence felt on the creative side. Dr. Landy had invited Lenny to the studio earlier and then Brian re-invited him again, saying "come on in and get your feet wet." Lenny knew that over twenty years had passed since the world had seriously paid attention to Brian...twenty years had passed since Brian had made an entire album worthy of serious attention. Lenny believed that everybody would ask one question---"Was this album worth the wait?" And that's why Lenny grew determined to get Brian to compose something unique like "Rio Grande."

"My background with Brian," Lenny explains "was loving the musicality of the hits, from 'Surfer Girl' to 'California Girls,' being amazed by Pet Sounds and then 'Good Vibrations,' which was, to me, the best single ever. It broke new ground; it was and is so bold. There are always moments as you grow up in the record business that affect you, and hearing 'Good Vibrations' for the first time was one of them. I was stunned by it."

Because of his creative association in 1966-1967 with Van Dyke Parks (Brian's Smile collaborator), Lenny was exposed to Brian's singular working process and 'was clearly taken by what he was attempting to do on that record. All the unreleased 'Smile' things, like the 'Heroes and Villains' Indian chanting, inspired 'Rio Grande' because I never forgot what I heard twenty years ago."

In 1970, the Beach Boys were signed to Reprise, and Lenny remembers being knocked out by "Cool Cool Water," a Smile relic that Brian refashioned for the Sunflower LP. "I just felt," Lenny emphasizes "that if Brian was going to make a record it would have to include something experimental, like the things he was doing before he went into hibernation. We had to have one."

What surprised Lenny was that when he approached Brian with the idea of trying something different, "Brian sort of resisted it. I thought it was gonig to be natural, that he would just go right for it. But, in fact, I think that the times he worked in that style were very painful for him, and he obviously wasn't anxious to relive them. As a matter of fact, we had a heated conversation. With Brian, a heated conversation is really one-sided, because you're the one that becomes heated.

"I was literally begging him to forget about pop ditties and 'song' songs. There were different times I talked to Brian about this. Brian would say 'OK,' and he would have a concept, like 'California,' but when he played it for me, it always ended up being a conventional song."

BRIAN WILSON

Part of the problem was that a record company president had never asked Brian for anything except hits. And now Lenn Waronker was trying to convince Brian to take a big creative chance.

"Lenny," Dr. Landy insists, "should get major credit for taking a major risk. He said, 'I want some art.' He could have had two more songs instead, two more chances at hits, and instead, he demanded that Brian stretch out artistically. 'Rio Grande' is 20% of the album, and it isn't something you can dance to. Lenny should be congratulated for pushing Brian in that direction."

Brian, whose musical reputation was on the line, calmly recalls that "Lenny wanted me to get a little bit into that kind of Smile bag, and I did. But at first, it was uncomfortable for me."

It was a pivotal meeting in late September that finally set "Rio Grande" in motion. Around the roaring fireplace at Brentwood's Country Mart, Lenny Waronker "scolded" Brian. "I said, 'I've had it. I'm not interested in songs. You've got to give me a piece of music. You have to try. You have nothing to lose.'

"Brian got flustered, asked for an idea, a thought. I said 'Write a cowboy song.' The reason for that was that there was virtually no way that could be a typical, conventional song. It forced his hand. It certainly wasn't an original idea of mine, because 'Heroes and Villains' was 'Cowboys and Indians.' But it seemed like the only way to get started.

"And then Brian said, 'Give me a title.' And I got flustered, because I'm not good at that. So we started flipping through some movie books that

I had bought that morning, and I thought of my favorite westerns. 'Red River' came up, which he liked, and then 'Rio Grande,' which he grabbed onto and kept."

On October 1st, the day a huge earthquake rocked the L.A. area, Brian Wilson with the assistance of Andy Paley began composing "Rio Grande." Within two weeks, they had the basic musical framework, and then Brian went into the studio to record it. Michael Bernard: "He sat down and played the whole thing, from front to back, just singing and playing his tack piano. Then, we started layering on top of that."

As Dr. Landy notes, before there was "Rio Grande," Brian had been working on a piece of music called "Life's Sweet," Brian's take on the cycles of life. Michael Bernard points out that "as it changed from being about life to 'Rio Grande,' it started to take on more of a three-dimensional effect. And so Brian asked me about sound effects to set up moods for different parts of the song. He wanted thunder and rain, which I had, but then he wanted separate water drops, a few here and there that you would hear like a big drop of water in a puddle. I went looking through sound effects libraries for those, and I found 'em." Before October was over, a rough track had been recorded.

Andy Paley, who co-wrote and co-produced "Rio Grande" with Brian, reveals Brian's philosophy behind the suite. "Brian was really into writing this as a survival thing, the idea of a little man against the big men and making it on your own...the misunderstandings that must have happened between travelers on the same trail and how scary that must have been."

Explaining their lyrical method, Andy points out that "Brian loves to play 'word association.' He would write a word down and hand me the pad, and I had to write a word down and hand it back to him. We got some phrases from that."

Naturally, Brian Wilson's "Rio Grande" isn't quite the same as the famous river. How did that happen? Andy Paley: "Many times, during the writing, we stopped and said, 'Were there Cherokees on the Rio Grande?' Probably not. But we liked the sound of Cherokee, so we used it. We didn't stop and say, 'What are we talking about? That never really happened.' That kind of thinking stifles creativity. We just went along and said that we'll go back and patch it up later, but later, we heard it and said, 'Why fix it? It sounds cool.'"

Throughout, Brian's ability to create mood with music came to the fore, particularly on segments like "Night Bloomin' Jasmine," when Brian would just get into a scary mood and write the melody in one take sitting at the keyboard. Lenny Waronker adds that the "Rain Dance" section "has that same kind of funny/scary Hitchcock-type paranoia. The vocal gymnastics, the ascending and descending notes, are all designed to make the listener feel what Brian is feeling, the theme of 'Rio Grande' which is all about fear and survival. Brian and Andy wrote the music and lyrics to create images and emotions that would express Brian's innermost feelings, the way his best music always has."

"So, on one hand, you have the lonely traveler, going down the 'Rio Grande,' afraid of what might happen to him, and then you finally get to the 'Take Me Home' section which is Brian reaching for safety and comfort. So the suite has a story, even though Brian didn't know for sure where it was leading when he started. He just followed his instincts down the river."

As Dr. Landy adds, "the original concept of 'Life's Sweet' was to use a river as a metaphor of life. So when Lenny and Brian came up with 'Rio Grande,' the same philosophy and feelings behind 'Life's Sweet' were utilized in the writing of 'Rio Grande.'"

Curiously, as complex as 'Rio Grande' sounds, it wasn't a difficult project for Brian. Lenny Waronker: "It really wasn't that tough. Brian's ideas were immediate; it was actually fun. That kind of musical excursion is fun. We don't get that often nowadays. This is a big canvas, and Brian, who has this incredible gift, has somehow put together a record that pays attention to almost all of the neat things, the different periods in his career, and he's done it in a modern way, ending up with something that is more than ambitious. I found myself looking forward to going into the studio with him because he moved so quickly.

"When you're with somebody who is that inspired, it's so great. He would say, 'I've got a thought,' and he'd go out and do it in the studio or use the emulator. Boom! One take. It was a producer's dream. Here, you've got this gigantic talent, and you sit there and say, 'How about this? How about that?' And he says, 'That's neat,' and he does it. Boom.

"And on 'Rio Grande,' anything that's not conventional worked so it was tremendous fun for me. I had done enough work with Van Dyke Parks to know some of the tricks he and Brian were messing with---any interesting folk-like instruments...harmonica, accordion, jew's harp---in fact, anything would work. Brian orchestrated the front of 'Rio Grande.' It has everything from water to flutes to oboes, an upright bass, a jug. It's an incredible orchestra. Probably, if it had been done with real musicians, you would have needed a 20-piece orchestra, and it would have been the most unusual 20-pieces you would ever see.

"It was relly wonderful to watch, because he did that in 'the good old days' with bass harmonica and god knows what kind of clusters. And here we're seeing him in the studio, and for once, the technology sped everything up. For me, it was this wonderful thing that I dreamed about for so long...watching this guy do his stuff. He didn't have to communicate his ideas to a player. He just sat at the emulator and did it. It was like magic."

Brian's favorite section of "Rio Grande" is "Take Me Home," and the vocals on that are a good example of the creative interplay that took place between Brian and Lenny.

"I kept wanting to change that section," Lenny recalls. "Brian was always most comfortable with 'Take Me Home,' but I wanted to do something. So I asked him if he could do some harmonies, a big cluster. We already had the background 'ooos,' but just one lead voice. I asked him if he could do a two or three-part harmony lead.

"And he figured out this real complex vocal thing that was way beyond what I would have come up with. He sat down at the piano and said, 'Here's what I would do.' And I said, 'Great,' as if I knew what the hell I was talking about.' He went out into the studio and did the four parts, the Four Freshmen. It wasn't that; it was something else. Whatever it was, I realized that 'Take Me Home' was very special.

BRIAN WILSON

"I think we needed some sort of repeatability in 'Rio Grande,' because it's pretty zany, and 'Take Me Home' gives it one hook. You know how every once in a while, we hear a song that has a great hook, and we'd love to hear that hook played over and over again? Forget going bck to the verse. Why do we have to wait? Let's just hear the hook. That's what 'Take Me Home' is. It's one hook, repeated four times. And what it hopefully does at that moment is drop you into a really neat harmonic place and leave you there for two minutes. And when Brian added those vocals, it seemed to lift not only that section but the entire track."

"Rio Grande" gave Lenny the ammunition he needed. "Now," he believed, "I had the record that would satisfy even the hardest core Brian Wilson fans and also show the critics that not only was Brian again writing wonderful songs but that he was beginning to stretch his creative muscles, that he was taking creative chances."

As Brian, Lenny and Andy labored in the studio to perfect "Rio Grande," Jeff Lynne (ELO's mastermind and architect of George Harrison's surprising comback LP) came to L.A. to work with Brian. Brian's music had been a major influence on Jeff, and when the two of them put their harmonic heads together the result was the wonderful "Let It Shine."

By Christmas of '87, the album had been recorded. After an extended holiday, Brian, Russ Titelman and ace mixer/engineer Hugh Padgham gathered at A&M's state-of-the-art studios for three weeks of mixing. Afterwards, determined to make his first solo album as good as possible, Brian followed up the first mixing sessions with a week of polishing. Because Brian only hears in one ear, he has never before mixed in stereo, and as <u>Brian Wilson</u>

is the first stereo album of his career, he wanted to take a little extra time to make sure that certain vocal and instrumental sounds weren't lost in the mix.

That tweaking done, the album was complete. At long last, in April of '88, one year after Brian had begun, the album was finished, and everybody sat back to assess their work. Russ Titelman: "It's truly incredible, a miracle. When Brian was doing it, he loved it. And when he finished, he was elated. When 'There's So Many' was done, he was smiling. And I was so overwhelmed by that cut, I said to him, 'I just want you to know how great I think this is, how great I think you're doing and how proud I am of you. I'm proud to be a part of this thing."

For Lenny Waronker, one of his favorite discoveries was to learn that "Brian really is an artist, a serious artist, very complex, very special. Working with him, I found him as a person to be considerate, kind, always sweet. As a collaborator, he's incredibly kind and generous. He has a way of taking an idea, no matter whose it is, and bending it in such a way that it works. And he doesn't even want to take the credit, that's how generous he is.

"What's really exciting is I sense that a lot of music is about to come out of him like an oil well that's about to blow. And I really think that this record shows that he's doing something special, something that's missing in tody's music, a unique palette of colors, sounds that only Brian can make."

From his point of view, having spent nearly six years working with Brian to bring him to this point, executive producer Dr. Eugene Landy points out that "everyone who worked on this record from the very beginning was very passionate and fully involved. The record has the distinction of so much input from all around, yet the integrity of the music is still 100% Brian Wilson."' Commenting on the creative ups and downs that are part of any project, Dr. landy wryly notes that 'actually, Brian has been the sanest of us all. Thoughout all the business and the bull, Brian has maintained his sense of purpose and come through it for himself and for all of us. Somehow, with our help, Brian has risen above us all and given us a great album."

BRIAN WILSON

BRIAN WILSON

...A Selected Discography

Top Forty Hits

All written, arranged and produced by Brian Wilson except where noted. Chart positions by <u>Billboard</u>.

Year	Title	Peak Position
1962	"Surfin' Safari"/"409"	#14/#76
1963	"Surfin' USA" */"Shut Down"	#3/#23
1963	"Surfer Girl"/"Little Deuce Coupe"	#7/#15
1963	"Be True To Your School"/"In My Room"	#6/#23
1964	"Fun, Fun, Fun"	#5
1964	"I Get Around"/"Don't Worry Baby"	#1/#24
1964	"When I Grow Up (To Be A Man)	#9
1964	"Dance, Dance, Dance"	#8
1965	"Do You Wanna Dance" **/"Please Let Me Wonder"	#12/#52
1965	"Help Me Rhonda"	#1
1965	"California Girls"	#3
1965	"The Little Girl I Once Knew"	#20
1966	"Barbara Ann" **	#2
1966	"Sloop John B." **	#3
1966	"Wouldn't It Be Nice"/"God Only Knows"	#8/#39
1966	"Caroline No"	#32

Sire Records · 75 Rockefeller Plaza · 20th Floor · New York, New York · 10019 · (212) 484-6870
Reprise Records, Inc. · 3300 Warner Boulevard · Burbank, California · 91510 · (818) 953-3223

BRIAN WILSON

Year	Title	Peak
1966	"Good Vibrations"	#1
1967	"Heroes & Villains"	#12
1967	"Wild Honey" ***	#31
1967	"Darlin'" ***	#19
1968	"Do It Again" ***	#20
1976	"Rock And Roll Music" *	#5
1976	"It's OK"	#29
1979	"Good Timin'" ***	#40
1982	"The Beach Boys Medley"	#12

*   Written by Chuck Berry, arranged and produced by Brian Wilson
** Arranged and produced by Brian Wilson
*** Written by Brian Wilson, produced by the Beach Boys

Top Twenty Albums

All arranged and produced by Brian Wilson.
Chart information by Billboard.
* indicates "Gold" album.

Year Released	Title	Peak Position	Weeks Charted
1963	* Surfin' U.S.A.	#2 (2 weeks)	78 weeks
1963	* Surfer Girl	#7	56 weeks
1963	* Little Deuce Coupe	#4	46 weeks
1964	* Shut Down, Vol. 2	#13	38 weeks
1964	* All Summer Long	#4	49 weeks
1964	* Beach Boys Concert	#1 (4 weeks)	62 weeks
1964	* Christmas Album	#6	3 weeks
1965	* Today!	#4	50 weeks
1965	* Summer Days (And Summer Nights!!!)	#2 (1 week)	33 weeks
1965	Party!	#6	24 weeks
1966	Pet Sounds	#10	39 weeks

BRIAN WILSON

Year	Album	Peak	Weeks
1966	* Best Of...	#8	78 weeks
1974	* Endless Summer	#1 (1 week)	155 weeks
1975	* Spirit Of America	#8	43 weeks
1976	* 15 Big Ones	#8	27 weeks

Top Twenty Hits

Written or co-written by Brian, recorded by other artists.

Year	Title	Artist	Peak Position
1963	"Surf City"	Jan & Dean	#1
1964	"Drag City"	Jan & Dean	#10
1964	"Dead Man's Curve"	Jan & Dean	#8
1964	"Little Honda"	The Hondells	#9
1977	"Don't Worry Baby"	B.J. Thomas	#17
1985	"California Girls"	David Lee Roth	#3

David Leaf, who researched and wrote this press kit, is the author of the acclaimed Brian Wilson biography, The Beach Boys & The California Myth.

BRIAN WILSON

STEPHEN SONDHEIM

DAVID BENOIT

BRIAN WILSON

CAROLE KING

the windham hill group

WINDHAM HILL RECORDS PUBLICITY
8750 Wilshire Blvd.
Beverly Hills, CA 90211

JAZZ GREATS ON VIDEO ③ Blakey, Ellington & More

TOWER RECORDS' PULSE!

BRIAN WILSON
Out of the Sandbox and Onto the Charts

- SONNY ROLLINS
- METALLICA
- JOSHUA BELL
- CINDERELLA

Plus: THE LYRES · ASWAD · VOIVOD · SHONA LAING
MICHELLE SHOCKED · ROTONDI · VOLCANO SUNS ·
MALCOLM'S INTERVIEW · THE CAT HEADS
COLIN NEWMAN

BRIAN WILSON

Shut Down Vol. 3

PHOTOGRAPH BY MARK HANAUER/ONYX

BRIAN WILSON

BY PAUL GREIN

IT'S BEEN A LONG ROAD BACK FOR BRIAN WILSON, CREATOR OF THE CALIFORNIA SOUND. HE RELEASED HIS FIRST SOLO ALBUM EVER EARLIER THIS YEAR, A CLASSIC PLATTER THAT RECALLS AN EARLIER ERA. YET THERE ARE STILL THOSE WHO DO NOT BELIEVE.

Malibu, Calif.

"The Beach Boys were my shell," states Brian Wilson, as he sprawls across the sofa in the living room of his Malibu home. "This album [Brian Wilson] symbolized my stepping out of the shell and going out there, kind of naked to the world. It was a hard thing for me to do. I'm amazed that I could do it."

Wilson isn't the only one who's amazed. Twenty-one years after this pop music legend decided not to release the Beach Boys' successor to Pet Sounds, the eagerly anticipated Smile, and began a long downward spiral of mental illness, drugs and diminishing involvement with Beach Boys' projects, he has finally released his first solo album, on Sire/Reprise Records. The album has received glowing reviews, which compare it to the Beach Boys' finest works.

Brian Wilson is definitely *not* Pet Sounds Vol. 2. It *is* the most consistently satisfying recording Wilson has attached his name to since Sunflower, the Beach Boys' 1970 debut for Brother/Reprise, however. Like Sunflower, the new album includes a number of well-crafted songs — "Love and Mercy," "Night Time," the extended suite "Rio Grande" and the exquisite "Melt Away" — which may not turn the pop music world on its collective ear (like "Good Vibrations" did), but which mark the return of a formidable talent many people had written off for good.

Wilson stares at the ceiling and admits that his reentry into the music business hasn't been easy.

"I'm scared, and I've been scared ever since we started this project," he confesses. "But being scared is natural. I know why I'm scared — because I don't want to fail."

Wilson, 46, is no stranger to fighting personal fears. He hit bottom in 1982, but since then, he has undergone a personal and professional transformation. He lost 130 pounds, swore off drugs and alcohol, and got back in touch with his substantial creative gifts.

"I was going down a long poison road," he admits, with the almost religious fervor of one who has been delivered from his demons. "I had to get in shape mentally to write these songs."

He rattles off a long list of his past sins: "Drugs, bad foods, no exercise, smoking, drinking. I was an alcoholic for many years. I don't do any of those things anymore. I feel great. I haven't felt this good since I was 24 — the year I made 'Good Vibrations.'"

Appropriately for Wilson, who crafted such unforgettable teen anthems as "Surfin' U.S.A." and "Surfer Girl," his home sits right next to the Pacific Ocean. The sound of waves crashing against the rocks is heard through the open sliding glass doors. The room is dimly lit by the late afternoon sun. Piles of CDs and tapes line the shelves, and a stack of *Billboards* sit on the coffee table.

Two of Wilson's aides work elsewhere in the house, but there is no publicist, no record company representative, no Dr. Eugene Landy — the controversial psychologist whose authoritarian regimen Wilson credits for his comeback — to hold his hand. Wilson is going it alone.

This man really *is* conquering his fears.

xxx

"I was thinking, 'Hey man, what's wrong with me? I can't seem to write a song here.'"

Wilson is recalling the dark years when he had lost touch with his talents.

"I'd plunk something out on the piano — 'Goddammit, no!' I'd shut the piano down. I'd take my fist and I'd bang the piano. I'd take my hands and just pound on the keys for a couple of minutes to try to get all that frustration out of me."

And this is Wilson's almost lyrical description of what it's like when the creative juices are flowing: "When the inspiration is really there, I look at the keys and it's magic. I say, 'I know this is going to be a song.' I feel it — you do this, you do that, you shuffle it around and all of a sudden you go, 'There! I've got a song written.'"

Over the years, Wilson has spent considerable time in both creative states of mind, and he's sure about one thing: It's a lot more fun when the magic is working.

In the long fallow stretch, Wilson says he rarely gave in to the fear that his talent had deserted him. "It was there. It was just lying dormant," he says. "It was unharnessed creativity. I had it inside of me. You never lose that."

The main problem was sheer exhaustion. "We [the Beach Boys] got worn out," Wilson admits. "We had been under pressure all those years to prove our greatness and to keep our place and our stature in the business. By 1972, we'd gotten to a point where we were a little bit fatigued. You could liken it to a pitcher full of water. You slowly pour the water out and finally there's no more water until you fill it back up."

But Wilson dismisses the widely held theory that his creative genius had become a burden. In fact, he says that, for him, being hailed as a genius was a plus.

"You're called a genius by people, and then your whole life you become the part," he explains. "Never has the genius aspect been a curse in my life. It's always been a source of strength. It's been a positive stroke in my life."

Wilson says that there were long periods in the '70s — two, three, four years — where he didn't write anything. And when he did try to "manufacture" a song, he wouldn't be happy with it. But he suggests that *not* writing violated his work ethic.

"You can't go two or three years without at least trying to write something, because that's your craft," he says. "A man has to work with his craft. It would be like a gardener going two years without mowing a lawn."

continued on 55

BRIAN WILSON

from 43

"The Beach Boys went from being a little stand-up bass/wire brush/one-guitar group all the way to a giant institution of American pop music. We're all proud of that. But none of us get along."

Every time Brian Wilson hears a great record, his competitive drive kicks into high gear.

"I say to myself, 'How could a guy create a record that great? It's like a kick in the ass. I relate to that kind of an idea. I relate to people being better than other people; saying this guy is better than this guy, and he's better than me at that. I can't help it — that's the way I am. I've been that way since I was born."

That fierce competitive streak helped Wilson achieve his greatest successes — but also was one of the central causes of his eventual burnout.

"When I was younger — when I did all the big Beach Boys albums — the competitive streak in me was under fire and I was just going mad," Wilson says. "I was out of my mind with competition."

But that competitive spirit was a positive force in Wilson's writing and production through the '60s. He would listen to the Beatles' **Rubber Soul** and be inspired to new heights on **Pet Sounds**, just as the Beatles would try to top **Pet Sounds** with **Sgt. Pepper's Lonely Hearts Club Band**.

"I didn't really see the negative side of competition until the early '70s," he says. "I remember in 1971, it started to just slide a little bit, I felt it slipping away. When I saw what was happening, it blew me away. I couldn't do it. I dropped out."

According to Wilson, the fierce competitive drive that fueled his work in the '60s came from just being young. "There's a fire burning inside a youth's body," he says. "It's the fire of youth. I call it the '20s people'. It's a boundless competitive urge; a crazy, fucked-up feeling that tells you much money over the years [1970-1978] that we were with them," he says, "but we were a prestigious act to have on the label. I think the label knows that I have the talent and the ability, and that I've proven in the past that I can get a hit."

The 11 songs on **Brian Wilson** were culled from 120 which Wilson had written in the last five years. "The idea was to create something that had a teeny bit of Beach Boys influence and yet was more my thing," he says. "It took us a year, because we worked at my pace. I told Dr. Landy I'd make a solo album if he let me do it at my own pace. He said, 'You've got a deal.'"

The album features several guest musicians, including Jeff Lynne, who teamed with Wilson to write and produce "Let It Shine," and Terence Trent D'Arby, who sang backup vocals on "Walkin' the Line."

D'Arby's role was originally going to be more prominent, Wilson says. "We had a hassle with CBS Records about his voice being used on my album. So we reduced it to a background singing part that wasn't distinguishable."

Wilson recorded most of his classic Beach Boys hits in three-track studios; he claims that modern recording technology intimidated him, at first. "I wasn't really too much into recording," he says, "but after the first month I saw how easy it was to work with synthesizer programmers and how they can achieve sounds that you never heard before.

"I think this new album is an indication that I've got it back," Wilson beams. "It's a cool album. It's good listening."

But he qualifies his review: "I value the record big hit? "I'd feel a little bad personally because no money [was] made there; no acclaim," he says. "I'd be a little disappointed because we spent a whole year making that album. You think I want to bomb after working a year? If it bombs, I might get pissed off. But I will not be crushed if it doesn't sell."

Maintaining that positive outlook, he says: "I'd probably go back and write some more songs and try another album." Wilson adds that if the album and a single from it both find their way into the Top 10, "it will be a lifetime thrill for me." The success in recent years of albums by veteran performers like Paul Simon, Steve Winwood and John Fogerty proves that there is at least a good chance that Wilson's album could be a major hit.

Wilson may support his album with a solo club tour. The decision hinges on the album's early success, but he says he's getting some songs choreographed just in case. "We won't have time to learn a whole show," he says. "We'll work up a few choreographed numbers and a couple of simple numbers and then just kind of play it by ear."

Some have suggested that Wilson may really hit his stride on his next album. The thinking is that a positive response to this debut will give Wilson the encouragement and confidence to advance to another level creatively. Wilson ponders the possibility, but seems reluctant to agree. He's been down this road before. "That's like when I said 'Heroes & Villains' was going to be better than 'Good Vibrations' and it wasn't — even though we put a lot of work into it," he says.

BRIAN WILSON

urge; a crazy, tucked-up feeling that tells you you've got to get out there and do it. You've got to stay up with the Joneses. You've got to win. You can't be called a loser," he says, spitting out the last word with disgust.

"If it gets too heavy, the kids drop out and the men go ahead," he adds. "The loser people drop out and the winner people keep going. When my name comes up, I just want people to say 'winner.'"

But his motivations were different when he wrote his current album. "This album was not born out of a competitive bag," he says. "I wrote these songs not in a competitive mood, but a musical mood."

xxx

Brian Wilson the album had its genesis in January 1987 at the Rock 'n' Roll Hall of Fame dinner in New York. Wilson was on hand to induct songwriters Jerry Leiber and Mike Stoller and was approached by Seymour Stein, president of Sire Records.

"There was a buzz going around that I was looking for a contract to do a solo album," Wilson recalls. "Seymour walked up to me and introduced himself and said he was interested in signing me. He met Gene [Landy], and before you know it, Seymour flew out to California to hear some of my songs. We agreed on certain songs, he gave us an opening budget and we started recording."

Wilson's affiliation with Sire/Reprise is his second time around with a Warner Bros. label; before the Beach Boys' unsuccessful eight-year stint with Caribou/CBS Records, the group's Brother label was distributed by Reprise.

"The Beach Boys didn't make Warner Bros. that but he qualifies his review: "I value the record as a production, but I don't think my voice sounds quite as alive as it has in the past," he confesses. "I'm self-conscious about my voice. When I hear it, I'm not satisfied. The spark is there, but I think some of the songs lay flat. It isn't my favorite album I ever recorded, but it is a good album. The next album will have a little more soul."

Wilson singles out two cuts as his favorites: The ballad "Melt Away" and the eight-minute suite "Rio Grande," which was based on a suggestion by Warner Bros. Records' president Lenny Waronker. "He said, 'Why don't you write a cowboy song called 'Rio Grande,'" Wilson says. "Then Dr. Landy stepped in and suggested writing a song with the first movement childhood, the second movement adolescence and the third movement adulthood. We tried that, but it fizzled out, so we went with Lenny's idea of writing a five- or six-part suite."

Despite Wilson's pride in such complex suites as "Heroes & Villains" and "Rio Grande," he plans to eschew longer-form pieces — rock operas, symphonies, film scores. His forte is the pop song, he insists, and that's what he'll stick with.

With the album in the stores, Wilson is anxious to see how it's going to be received. "An album can flop on its ass — just sort of sit there like a heavy rock in the sand," he says. "That might be what happens to my album. I know I *want* to have a hit record, but I don't have that big a chance. My name personally isn't that big with the public — especially with the new generation. Eighty percent of the sales of the Hot 100 records are to kids under 20. That's the biggest market."

How would Wilson react if the album wasn't a "The Beach Boys have come a long way from where we started," Wilson says proudly. "We've gone from being a little stand-up bass/wire brush/one-guitar group all the way to a giant institution of American pop music. We're all proud of that. But none of us get along.

"That's the great balance, right? You couldn't have that successful a group and have us all get along. You'd have to have inter-group conflicts as a built-in price for our success and our fame."

There's nothing new about reports of tension in the Beach Boys, but what is new is Wilson's ability to handle that tension. The main way he's coping, it appears, is to simply avoid it.

He says he may perform a few concert dates a year with the group, but he won't undertake any extended tours. Likewise, he may produce a couple of songs, but not any full-length album projects.

"There are so many mixed feelings in the Beach Boys that I can't handle it," he says. "I don't like it. I don't like the way it feels, so I just canned it and said that I don't want to do very many shows with them."

The bottom line for Wilson: "I stopped worrying about Mike Love and Carl Wilson and those guys, and started worrying about myself. If there's a fight, that would be very discomforting, but if there is, there is."

Clearly, the tensions within the Beach Boys run very deep.

"When I show up to a concert, I feel their resentment," Wilson says. "I feel like they think, 'Oh, he gets to come out whenever he wants to, but we have to work all year.' Little do they know I'm under just as much pressure as they are.

Wilson says. "He asks, 'What's happening?' 'Let's have a detailed report.'" Kevin [Leslie, Wilson's live-in aide] brings [Landy] up to date on what's happened since we last talked to him."

Wilson becomes visibly agitated when discussing the media's widespread ridicule of Landy. "I think he takes a lot of shit from writers and from my family and that he's been treated unfairly," he says. "They're not getting the full picture of what really happened with me and Dr. Landy — just part of the picture. They're uninformed as to what has really occurred. I feel bad about it. I feel bad for Gene because he has to sit there and take that shit. He doesn't deserve it. He deserves more credit than he's getting."

Wilson readily agrees with the suggestion that Landy is a parental figure to him, but he also indicates that he looks forward to the day — "I hope within the next year" — that he'll be weaned from Landy's control and start making his own decisions.

In fact, Wilson suggests that he feels ready to break away now. "I have for a couple of months now," he says, "but it's not going to get anywhere. I haven't even asked him if I can leave the program, but I know I can't. I think I'm ready to leave, but maybe it might take another year to leave, to have my own independent life back."

Who will make the decision about leaving Landy? "Gene will. Gene will make it. I won't."

But how can you be ready to take your life into your own hands if you have to ask permission from someone else to do so? "I don't know," says Wilson softly. "I really don't want to talk about it. This is sort of like a closed subject right now. It's not something that can be resolved."

Twenty minutes later, the phone rings. Before anyone answers it, Wilson says: "That's Gene calling. That's Dr. Landy calling."

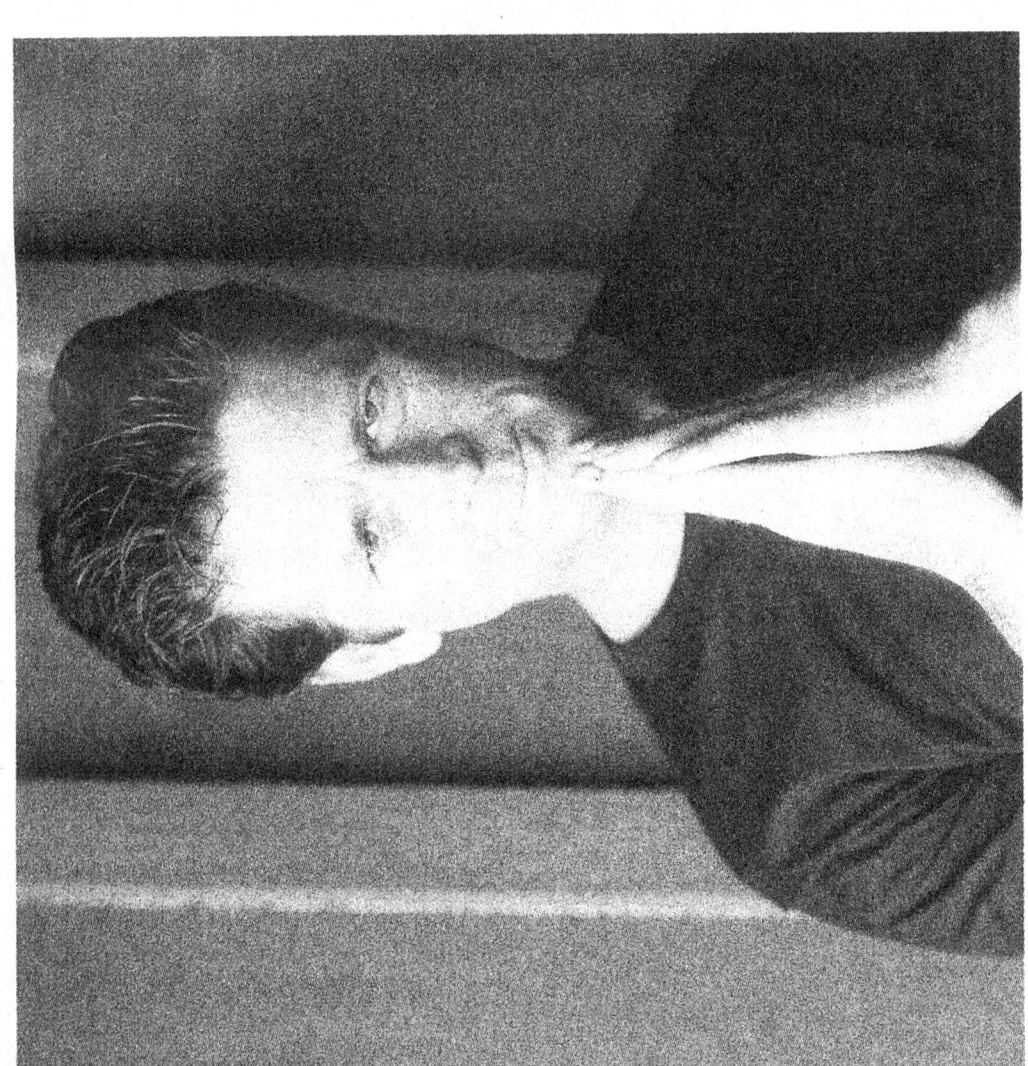

"I think the Beach Boys are playing fear-games with me," Wilson adds. "They write letters to Gene [Landy] and other people saying, 'We don't think Brian should get his share [of concert income] because he's not on the road.' It makes me feared-out. They know it's going to fear me out when they do that because their touring is my only source of income."

How does Wilson figure he deserves a share of the group's concert receipts? Simple. Without Brian Wilson's music, there would *be* no Beach Boys.

"If it's going to come to those kind of games, I'll bow out entirely," he says. "I will not participate in a group that plays games like that. If they tell me to my face they want to do something with me [that's one thing], but if it's through letters to Gene and other people, I won't do it. I'd rather just go in and do my second album and fuck off with the Beach Boys. It's not worth it to me to go through that much shit."

Wilson acknowledges that he isn't the only one in this situation to feel frustration.

"The Beach Boys probably feel a little shackled, too, when every night they've got to do '409' and 'Shut Down' and 'Surfin' Safari.' They have to do all those songs and they hate it, but that's what made 'em famous so they've got to do it. I think the guys would much rather do some of the album cuts that we've done over the years, but they do those old songs that sound for shit. They sound real stupid."

The tensions in the group have led to some puzzling career decisions. In the late '70s and early '80s, when they clearly could have used a hit, the Beach Boys shelved what Wilson considers one of their best songs, "Boys, Girls."

"It was a hell of a commercial little song, but we threw it in the can," he says. "We never did anything with it."

Why not? "I don't know," Wilson answers. "Everyone just got crazy. It got all screwed up. We sort of felt sour grapes about what was happening with us. The **L.A. (Light Album)** didn't sell and it had a fuckin' great couple of songs on it. We were looking for a big record with that one. That set us back a little bit when that album bombed."

The most controversial aspect of the Brian Wilson story is surely his near-total reliance on one Dr. Eugene E. Landy. Wilson started seeing Landy, a psychologist whose methods have been called into question by his colleagues on more than one occasion, in 1976, the year the Beach Boys released their comeback album, **15 Big Ones**. That initial association lasted a few years; after six years apart, Landy and Wilson resumed their association in January 1983. Landy has called the shots in Wilson's life ever since.

"Dr. Landy is my daily planner, my executive producer, my lyric-writing partner and my business partner," Wilson says. "He's the sole person who got me back. It was all his doing."

Would Wilson go so far as to say that Landy saved his life? "Absolutely," he insists. "I still learn from him. He still teaches me things."

Wilson suggests that their relationship mirrors the credits on the new album. "He's the executive producer, which is higher on the totem pole than producer."

Landy exerts this tremendous influence over Wilson through the use of a controversial 24-hour-a-day monitoring program. "He checks all the time during the day, up to when I go to bed at night,"

In conversation, Brian Wilson often seems befuddled and confused. He brings to mind the innocent man-child portrayed on stage by Tommy Smothers. At first it seems sweet and endearing, then almost comic, and ultimately sad and frightening. But you have to respect Wilson: He's clearly struggling to get by the best he can.

You find yourself giving him pep talks, trying to boost his fragile ego. He may lack confidence and certain social skills, you reason, but he's a good kid with a lot of heart — a lot like a typical eighth-grader. He even talks like an eighth-grader, peppering his conversation with schoolyard slang and obscenities.

While most pop stars keep their guard up in interviews and reveal only as much about their personal lives as they choose to, Wilson freely discusses his private life.

For example, he comments openly about the causes of his three nervous breakdowns in the 1960s. "By that time I was a legend and I had trouble dealing with people as a person and not a star," he says. "I began to think that people only liked me because I was famous. I felt like I couldn't trust anybody in the whole world. I couldn't trust people with my feelings. Every time I turned around, I'd get my feelings hurt. The fact that I didn't trust people drove me nuts. I kind of broke down. I cracked up."

Wilson's stance throughout the interview — laying down on the sofa — may contribute to his confessional outpouring. His interviewers, perhaps, become surrogate Dr. Landys.

But at other points, he seems very much in command. Ask him a general question about drug use in the '60s that he doesn't want to answer, and he

continued on 68

BRIAN WILSON
from 56

declines in a way that shuts the door to follow-up questions without making him seem defensive. "My well's gone dry on this one subject," he says. "I don't know how to approach the answer, so I'll pass it."

Wilson occasionally displays a good — if oddball — sense of humor. Referring to Mike Love, the Beach Boys' controversial lead singer, Wilson says: "He's a great singer, a great emcee and a great-looking guy. Unfortunately, he does have a little bit of a problem with his hair, but that's just to keep him going. You know why God did that to him, don't you? So he won't quit. So he'll be tough and say, 'Goddamn! I'm going to get this right if it kills me.'"

Wilson employs religious imagery often in the conversation. He suggests that his nervous breakdowns were "triggered by the devil himself." Later, he said that his creative block "could have been a mistake by God."

At times Wilson's manner is so dry that it's hard to tell if he is kidding or not. Talking about the prospects for his record, he blurts out: "I think it might take some payola." Come again? "I think it might take a little payola in order to get enough airplay to get a hit."

> "The idea was to create something that had a teeny bit of Beach Boys influence, and yet was more my thing."

At another point, he asks if I'd seen a particular Beach Boys' TV special. Told, no I hadn't, he pauses briefly and then explodes: "Damn!" It was impossible to know if it was mock, exaggerated disapproval — a dry parody of a star tantrum — or the real thing.

xxx

Wilson has been a student and fan of pop music since he was a teenager growing up in Hawthorne, Calif. Then, he listened to KFWB-AM and doted on hits by the Four Freshmen and producer Phil Spector.

Wilson says that he has continued to listen to the radio through the years and has always found something that he liked — except for one stretch a decade ago. "The big disco push in the late '70s drove me nuts," he said, "except for that 'Boogie Woogie Dancin' Shoes,' [a 1979 hit for Claudia Barry]. That was my favorite, and the Bee Gees' records were great, too.

Wilson remains a pop buff. "Charts are fascinating," he said. "You open up *Billboard* and say, 'Wow — I wonder what will be the number one record of the week.' George Michael went to number one a couple of weeks ago. I love his record, 'One More Try.'"

What else has Wilson liked in the last few years? He quickly names "Man In Motion (Theme from 'St. Elmo's Fire')," the John Parr movie hit, but then draws a blank.

We toss out some obvious possibilities to get his reaction.

● Michael Jackson — "Yeah. 'She's Out of My Life' — great record."

● Prince — "I never really took a liking to Prince that much."

● Phil Collins — "Yeah, I met him. I met Michael Jackson too."

● Madonna — "I'm trying to think. No ... Yeah. Madonna is on the same label I am. Yeah. I do like her stuff."

● The Beach Boys — "I like their hits; some of them I love — especially 'Good Vibrations' and 'California Girls.'"

But Wilson says he isn't fond of other Beach Boys songs.

"We made a plastic, contrived record here and there," he says. "I think we're respected as a group that made good records, but there are records that I'm sorry I put my name on."

xxx

add. Artists almost always say, "No, I think we've covered things pretty well." Occasionally they clarify one point that may have been glossed over.

Wilson, however, is a different story: "Yeah, I'd like to say a few things," he says, shifting into an upright position for the first time in the two-hour interview.

"In closing," he begins, "I'd like to establish the fact that I want people to know that I am 100 percent behind the health movement that's going on in this country. A small percentage of people are exercising a lot more nowadays as you may have noticed. Also, there's a growing concern about red meat. There's a growing awareness that health foods and healthy foods have a connection with how well your brain functions. I just want people to know that I endorse these areas.

"Exercise is something that most people don't have time for. A guy says, 'Why should I get up at five in the morning and exercise before work? I need the sleep.' Or, 'Why should I spend my precious leisure time on a weekend exercising?' With those excuses, he's shot down. He's either too lazy or he just doesn't want to make it his lifestyle to eat right or exercise. But for those people who can find time for it, I condone exercise as a way of life that is very, very good for the brain.

"That is all I want to say." ●

BRIAN WILSON

on record
WORDS | ABOUT | SOUNDS

Out of the Sandbox
Brian Wilson's return to semi-greatness

Brian Wilson
Imagination
(Giant)
★★★

Brian Wilson fans have been hearing false alarms to the tune of "Brian's back!" since 1976. So skepticism is the only sensible response to the comeback hype accompanying the release of *Imagination*, the former Beach Boys genius' first album of new songs in a decade.

It certainly isn't encouraging to hear that Wilson's co-producer and main collaborator here is MOR schlockmeister Joe Thomas, who masterminded the gawd-awful 1996 Beach Boys country "tribute" *Stars and Stripes* (on Thomas' River North label). Or that Wilson's co-writers include such noted hacks as Jimmy Buffett, J.D. Souther, Carole Bayer Sager and Survivor's Jim Peterik. Or that three of the album's 11 tracks are remakes of old Beach Boys numbers.

So it's both a letdown and a relief to report that *Imagination* is neither a brilliant return to form nor a crushing embarrassment. It's a generally respectable, frequently enjoyable effort on which Wilson sounds engaged and in control, if not necessarily inspired. It's understandable that Wilson, working with these less-than-challenging co-workers, wouldn't feel compelled to push the envelope. So it shouldn't be big news that nothing on *Imagination* approaches the musical invention and emotional depth of the artist's best work, and that the album's successes generally have more to do with craft than innovation.

The airily effervescent "Your Imagination" opens the album on a gently uplifting note, showcasing Wilson's multi-tracked vocals, whose impressive arrangements compensate somewhat for his inexact phrasing. The dreaded Buffett co-write "South American" is actually an amiable tropical trifle, and the similarly breezy "Dream Angel" and "Sunshine" are enjoyably lightweight. The heartfelt "Lay Down Burden" has a bittersweet if underdeveloped autobiographical edge, as does the ambitious album-closer "Happy Days." But "Cry" squanders a lovely melody on Brian's own sappy lyrics, and "Where Has Love Been?" is unredeemably bathetic.

Elsewhere, "She Says That She Needs Me" resurrects the unreleased (though much-bootlegged) vintage Beach Boys tune "Sherry She Needs Me" in a revamped version—with lyrics awkwardly rewritten by Sager—that lacks the original's majestic urgency. A

BRIAN WILSON

on record

new reading of the early Beach Boys track "Keep an Eye on Summer" now registers as a poignant meditation on lost innocence, but an unspectacular remake of the 1965 classic "Let Him Run Wild" can't help but pale in comparison to the original's magnificence.

Given his troubled history, the fact that Brian Wilson is still making music at all is a remarkable accomplishment. Perhaps the biggest compliment that can be paid *Imagination* is that, unlike 1988's underwhelming *Brian Wilson*, it leaves one eager to hear the artist's next album—and confident that we won't have to wait another decade for it. —BY SCOTT SCHINDER

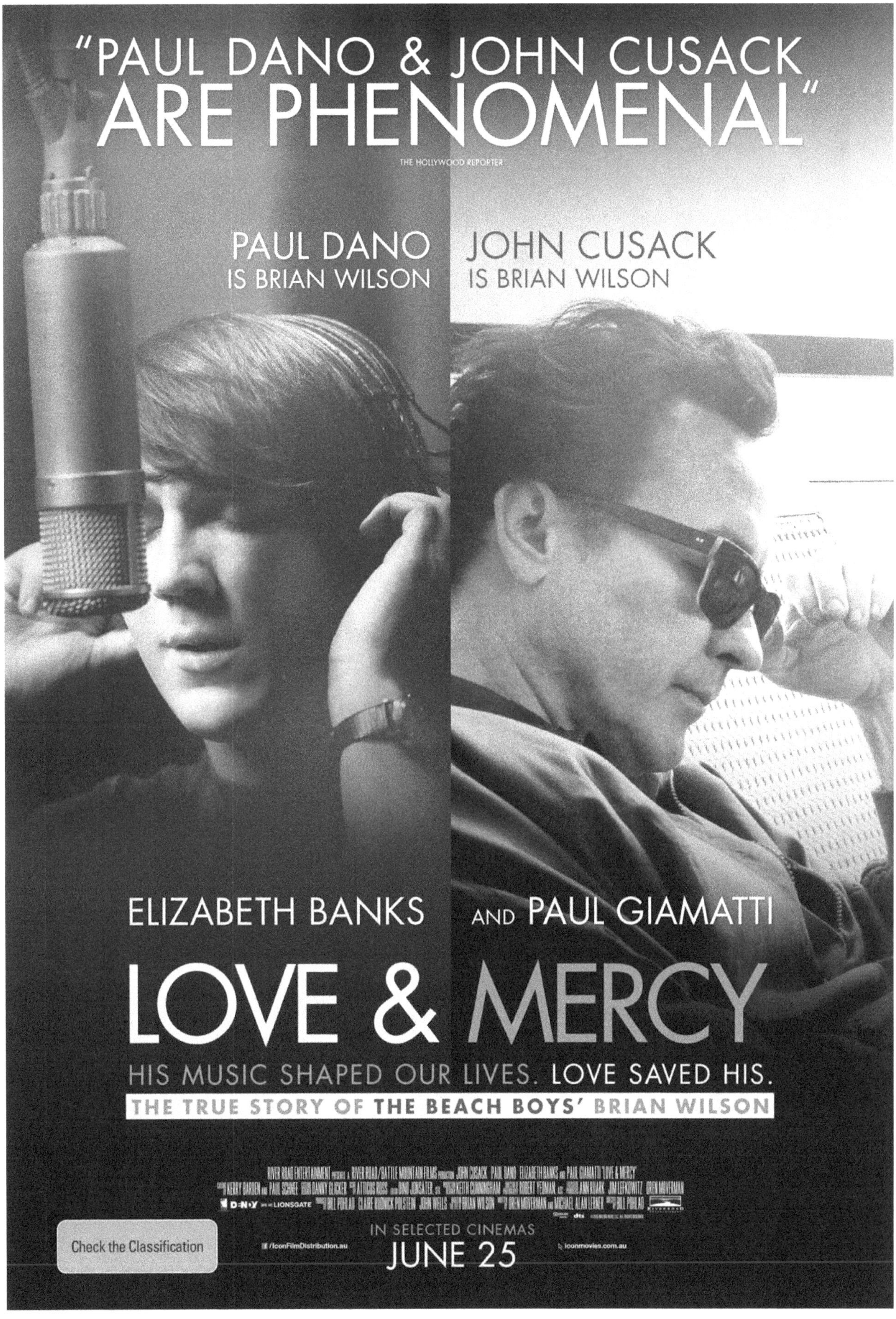
"PAUL DANO & JOHN CUSACK
ARE PHENOMENAL"
THE HOLLYWOOD REPORTER
PAUL DANO
IS BRIAN WILSON
JOHN CUSACK
IS BRIAN WILSON
ELIZABETH BANKS AND PAUL GIAMATTI
LOVE & MERCY
HIS MUSIC SHAPED OUR LIVES. LOVE SAVED HIS.
THE TRUE STORY OF THE BEACH BOYS' BRIAN WILSON
Check the Classification
IN SELECTED CINEMAS
JUNE 25

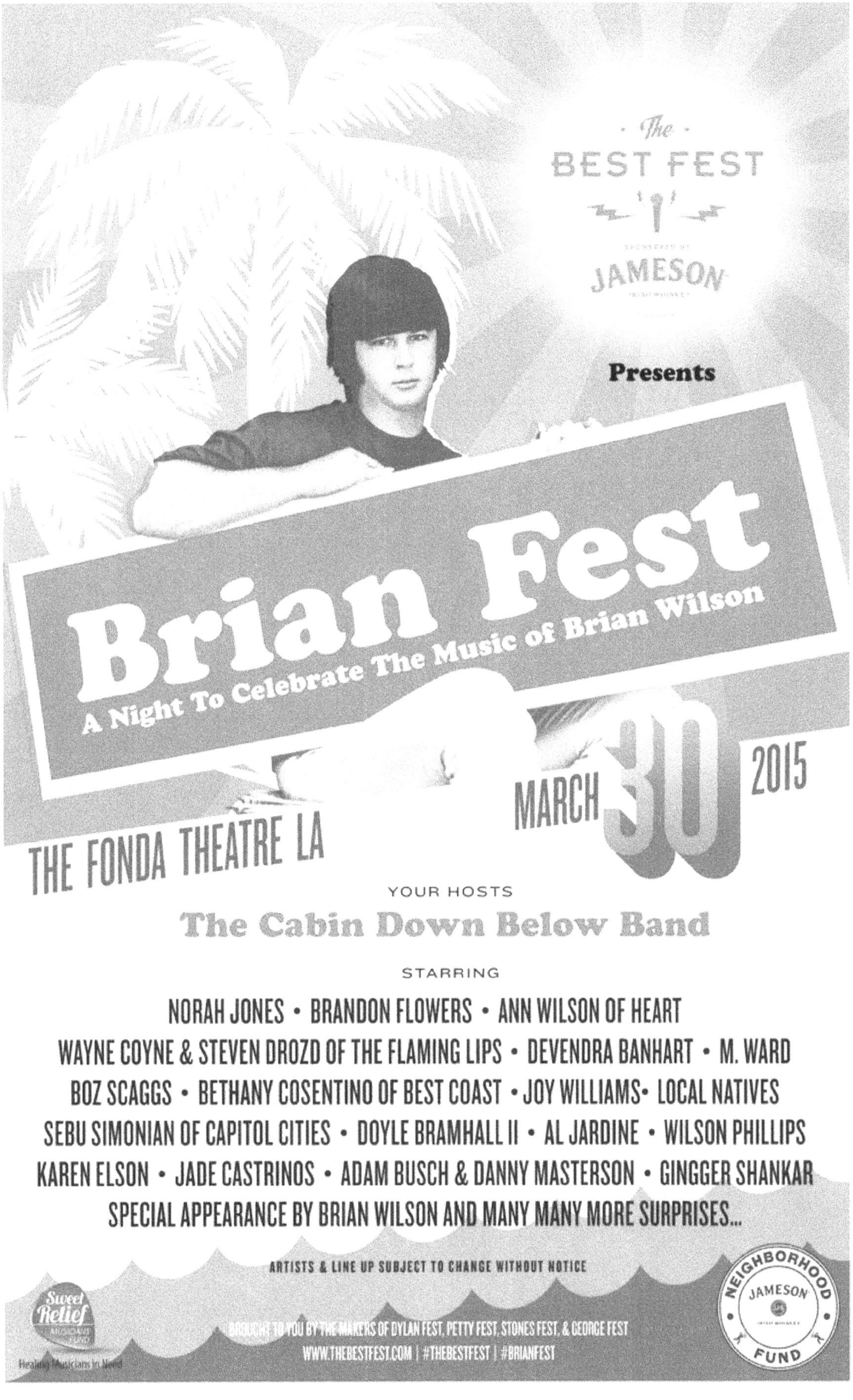
The
BEST FEST
JAMESON
Presents
Brian Fest
A Night To Celebrate The Music of Brian Wilson
MARCH 30 2015
THE FONDA THEATRE LA
YOUR HOSTS
The Cabin Down Below Band
STARRING
NORAH JONES • BRANDON FLOWERS • ANN WILSON OF HEART
WAYNE COYNE & STEVEN DROZD OF THE FLAMING LIPS • DEVENDRA BANHART • M. WARD
BOZ SCAGGS • BETHANY COSENTINO OF BEST COAST • JOY WILLIAMS• LOCAL NATIVES
SEBU SIMONIAN OF CAPITOL CITIES • DOYLE BRAMHALL II • AL JARDINE • WILSON PHILLIPS
KAREN ELSON • JADE CASTRINOS • ADAM BUSCH & DANNY MASTERSON • GINGGER SHANKAR
SPECIAL APPEARANCE BY BRIAN WILSON AND MANY MANY MORE SURPRISES...
ARTISTS & LINE UP SUBJECT TO CHANGE WITHOUT NOTICE
Sweet Relief
Healing Musicians in Need
BROUGHT TO YOU BY THE MAKERS OF DYLAN FEST, PETTY FEST, STONES FEST, & GEORGE FEST
WWW.THEBESTFEST.COM | #THEBESTFEST | #BRIANFEST
NEIGHBORHOOD
JAMESON
FUND

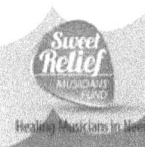

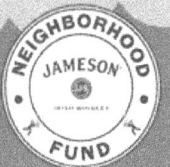

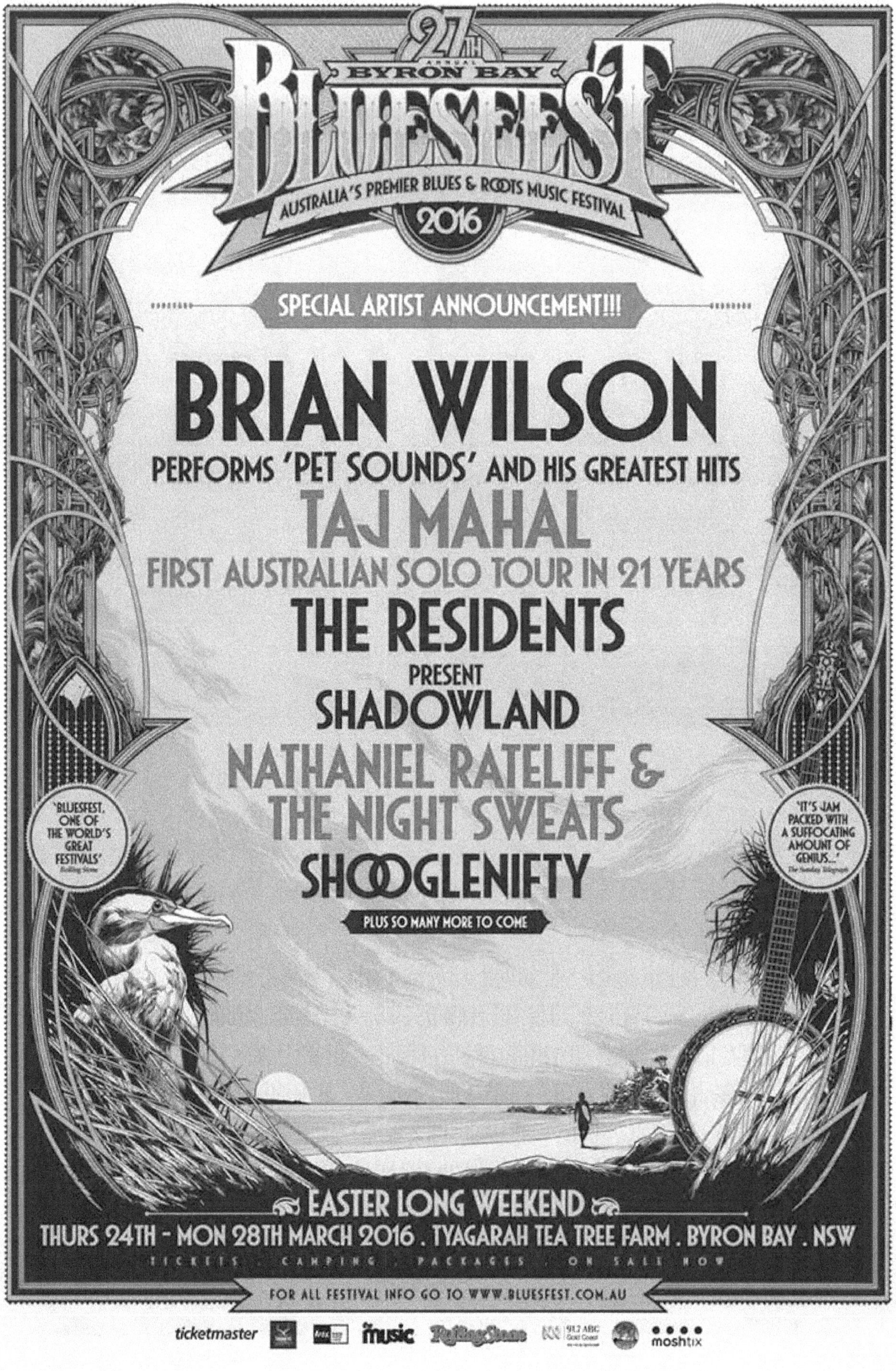
27TH ANNUAL
BYRON BAY
BLUESFEST
AUSTRALIA'S PREMIER BLUES & ROOTS MUSIC FESTIVAL
2016
SPECIAL ARTIST ANNOUNCEMENT!!!
BRIAN WILSON
PERFORMS 'PET SOUNDS' AND HIS GREATEST HITS
TAJ MAHAL
FIRST AUSTRALIAN SOLO TOUR IN 21 YEARS
THE RESIDENTS
PRESENT
SHADOWLAND
NATHANIEL RATELIFF &
THE NIGHT SWEATS
SHOOGLENIFTY
PLUS SO MANY MORE TO COME
'BLUESFEST, ONE OF THE WORLD'S GREAT FESTIVALS'
'IT'S JAM PACKED WITH A SUFFOCATING AMOUNT OF GENIUS...'
EASTER LONG WEEKEND
THURS 24TH - MON 28TH MARCH 2016 . TYAGARAH TEA TREE FARM . BYRON BAY . NSW
TICKETS . CAMPING . PACKAGES . ON SALE NOW
FOR ALL FESTIVAL INFO GO TO WWW.BLUESFEST.COM.AU
ticketmaster
moshtix

BRIAN WILSON